Avro Vulca[n] 2

A Place in History, 1960–84

DAVID W. FILDES

HISTORIC MILITARY AIRCRAFT SERIES, VOLUME 19

Contents page image: Pictured here is Avro Vulcan XM603 in its camouflage scheme before it was repainted in its all-white anti-flash scheme. It can now be seen at the Avro Heritage Museum at Woodford, where it was built.

David W Fildes joined Hawker Siddley Aviation in 1972 after working in the advertising industry. He joined the Publicity Department at Chadderton and later moved to Woodford. This is where he found an association with the XM603 Club, and later formed the Avro Hertiage Centre, with the help of Dr Peter Summerfield and Harry Holmes. It is now known as the Avro Heritage Museum, based at Woodford, and is home to XM603, shown here in the background.

Published by Key Books
An imprint of Key Publishing Ltd
PO Box 100
Stamford
Lincs PE9 1XQ

www.keypublishing.com

The right of David W. Fildes to be identified as the author of this book has been asserted in accordance with the Copyright, Designs and Patents Act 1988 Sections 77 and 78.

Typeset by SJmagic DESIGN SERVICES, India.

Acknowledgements

To my friend and colleague Harry Holmes for his support and encouragement over the years. Also to Tony Blackman, Reg Boor, Ian Lowe, Ken Newby and George Lee, who gave some useful advice.

Dedication

I would like to dedicate this book to members of the XM603 Club, who were retired members that had worked on the Avro Vulcan XM603 at Woodford since 1985. In 2007, the club members were stood down when their numbers started to deplete, and others became too old to support the aircraft. Their legacy still continues today in the Avro Heritage Museum at Woodford where XM603 can be seen.

I would also like to recognise the contributions made by the workforce at both Chadderton and Woodford and their dedication in producing one of the world's most iconic aircraft, and to the pilots and crews who flew the Vulcan.

Contents

The last Vulcan to fly, XH558, and the first B.Mk2 delivered to the Royal Air Force (RAF) in July 1960.

Dawn of the Thermonuclear Age

Design of the United Kingdom's first plutonium bomb began in June 1947 in response to an Air Ministry requirement, OR.1001, issued in August 1946. Based at Fort Halstead in Kent under (Sir) William Penney, a nuclear research programme was started known as High Explosive Research (HER). This led to a nuclear test under the code name 'Hurricane', which had shown that Britain had mastered the design of a plutonium atomic bomb. This design was adopted for Britain's first nuclear bomb, known as Blue Danube. It was delivered to the RAF in 1953 but only given its certificate of airworthiness (C[A]) approval in 1957.

In 1952, Aldermaston had become the home for the Atomic Weapons Research Establishment (AWRE) – the same year America first tested a thermonuclear weapon, followed shortly after by the Soviet Union. A hydrogen or thermonuclear weapon uses a fission bomb to start a fusion reaction; these weapons are more powerful than nuclear fission weapons. In 1954 the United Kingdom decided to develop a hydrogen bomb.

In 1956, a series of tests were performed under the code name Operation *Buffalo*, using both weapons-grade plutonium and uranium-235. This was later to become the Red Beard tactical nuclear bomb. The Red Beard design concept was similar to the Blue Danube warhead, but the overall size was reduced thanks to its innovative means of implosion. Red Beard entered RAF service in 1962. In parallel, work was commencing on a true thermonuclear device.

Between 1957 and 1958, the UK performed a series of thermonuclear tests known as the *Grapple* series. A hybrid weapon known as Green Bamboo was intended as the warhead for all proposed projected delivery systems; this included the Yellow Sun and Avro Blue Steel missile. Green Bamboo and Green Granite were both interim thermonuclear designs that proved to be large and heavy, so a smaller sphere was designed that led to Orange Herald, which was a large boosted fission weapon of reduced size and yield.

When the V-bomber force entered service, the Valiant, Victor and Vulcan were armed with the non-thermonuclear Blue Danube nuclear bomb. Early attempts of a high-yield nuclear bomb led to Violet Club (using a Green Grass warhead in a Blue Danube casing), which was provided in a limited supply that was only used in Avro Vulcan aircraft. Violet Club was deployed in 1958 until it was replaced by the Yellow Sun nuclear bomb using the Green Grass 'Granite' warhead. Yellow Sun referred to the outer casing, which was designed to contain a variety of warhead designs and entered service in 1959.

On 2 July 1958, President Eisenhower signed amendments to the 1954 United States Atomic Energy Act. This led to a bilateral agreement between Britain and America on nuclear weapon design information. The UK designers redesigned the American Mk28 two-stage warhead that became known as Red Snow and fitted it to the Yellow Sun casing. The Yellow Sun Mk2 saw service between 1961 and 1972 and, like the Avro Blue Steel air-launched missile was also fitted with the Red Snow physics package.

The much safer Yellow Sun Mk2 was regarded as Britain's first true thermonuclear weapon and began to replace the Yellow Sun Mk1 in 1962. Yellow Sun was used alongside the American Mk5 atomic bomb under the shared Project E programme from 1957 until sufficient British nuclear weapons became available; the American Mk5 nuclear weapon was phased out in 1962.

Later, the development of a new thermonuclear bomb was designed to be used by the TSR-2 (tactical strike and reconnaissance) aircraft. Known as the WE177, it had a lightweight warhead design that could be used at both high- and low-level flight and was used by a variety of aircraft including the Vulcan. It started to replace Red Beard in the early 1970s. The first WE117 Type B was delivered to the RAF at Cottesmore in September 1966. The WE117 was finally withdrawn in 1998, leaving the RAF without a nuclear capability.

A number of companies were involved in designing and testing bomb casings, delivery systems, electronics, and radar and arming fusing and firing mechanisms. The Royal Aircraft Establishment (RAE) at Farnborough co-ordinated much of the design work and the RAE at Boscombe Down conducted flight trials.

The United Kingdom's nuclear deterrent is now carried by the Royal Navy submarine fleet and comprises a warhead design compatible with the American Trident Strategic Weapons System, which can be used in both the strategic and sub-strategic roles by altering the warhead yields.

Avro, the Company

The last production Vulcan was manufactured in 1964 and delivered in 1965, and was still supported and modified by the Hawker Siddeley Aviation/British Aerospace sites at Chadderton and Woodford during its service life.

The Duncan Sandys White Paper on Defence in March 1957 stated there would be no more piloted military aircraft. This led to the cancellation of the Avro Type 730 reconnaissance and strategic bomber. The Avro Type 730 was to carry the Blue Rosette short-case nuclear bomb, using the Green Bamboo or Orange Herald nuclear device. Blue Rosette was cancelled in April 1957, and, in the same year, Avro decided to re-enter the civil market. This led to the design of the successful Avro 748 turboprop airliner, which chief test pilot Jimmy Harrison first flew on 24 June 1960.

Avro Type 730 with ECM drone.

In 1963, the Avro name was dropped when the company became part of the Hawker Siddeley Aviation Group. Later, in 1977, it became part of British Aerospace, which, in 1999, became known as BAE Systems. In 1993 British Aerospace resurrected the Avro name to consolidate assembly of the 146 short-haul and regional airliner at Woodford. The sites at Chadderton and Woodford were kept busy with the 748/Andover, Victor tanker conversion, Nimrod, Airbus, 146/RJ and Advanced Turboprop (ATP) airliner programmes. The ATP eventually went to the Prestwick site and became known as the Jetstream 64. Following the cancellation of the RJX airliner and Nimrod programmes, it was decided, in 2011, to close the BAE Systems sites at Chadderton and Woodford.

Exterior mock-up of the Avro 748 at Chadderton on 26 November 1958.

Chadderton and Woodford products 1960–2011

The Avro Vulcan B.Mk2 entered service in 1960. Pictured is XH558, which last flew in 2015.

The Avro 748 first flew in 1960. More than 380 were built, with 322 sold worldwide.

The Avro Shackleton first flew in 1949. The AEW version entered service in 1972 and retired in 1991.

The British Aerospace ATP first flew in 1986. Its manufacture ended in 1996 at Woodford.

The Avro RJX was a development of the 146/RJ family of aircraft. It first flew in April 2001 but in December that year BAE Systems cancelled the project.

The Nimrod's first flight was in 1967. A new version, the Nimrod MRA4, first flew in 2009 but was later cancelled in 2010.

Chadderton and Woodford sites

The Chadderton site photographed on 27 July 1991. It is now home to Mono Pumps Ltd.

Woodford site taken on 1 August 1991. It is now a garden village and home to the Avro Heritage Museum.

The Avro Vulcan B.Mk2

I n June 1955, an Avro report looked at the potential development of the Vulcan B.Mk1 along with the requirement to carry a stand-off missile that later became known as Blue Steel.

A brochure issued in March 1956 described the aircraft as a high-altitude long-range bomber powered by four Olympus B.01.6 jet engines of 16,000 or 16,500lb each, depending on which engines were installed. Also quoted were four Rolls-Royce Conway stage-3 jet engines, developing 16,500lb at sea-level static thrust. Cruising altitude was quoted as being 45,000ft–65,000ft with a cruising speed of 500 knots. Range with a standard 10,000lb load was 5,000nm or 5,500nm with a 13,000lb special store. Provision was to be made for serial aerial refuelling, either as a tanker or receiver. The gross weight had increased to 190,000lb. A full structural strength testing programme was being undertaken at the time the brochure was printed, and calculations showed the specified weight of 190,000lb would be fully met.

The wingspan had increased to 111ft, and a new AC electrical system fitted. Another major change was made to the flying controls from elevators and ailerons. These were in the form of four elevons split outboard and inboard on each wing. The term 'elevon' was an amalgamation of 'elevator' and 'aileron'. Missing from the brochure was the new electronic counter measure (ECM) kit fitted to later B.Mk1A aircraft.

An artificial stability system was included in the form of a pitch damper system, to be used at altitudes in excess of 20,000ft. An auto-Mach-trim system was introduced to counteract the tendency towards instability and designed to leave the pilot with the impression of an aircraft with positive static stability throughout. The natural stability of the aircraft in yaw was supplemented by the introduction of a yaw-damping system to fulfil the stringent requirements of the aircraft's various roles.

Also mentioned was reference to a special store weighing 13,000lb; no illustration was included in the brochure.

When the Vulcan B.Mk2 version was proposed, a new wing leading edge modification was designed. The 'Phase 2C' wing as it was known was allotted to be fitted to VX777 and contract 6/Aircraft/13262/CB.6(a) was issued for an aerodynamic prototype.

Shown below is the second prototype Vulcan, VX777, taking off from Woodford on an early test flight.

Summary

The June 1955 report stated that the aerodynamic testing of the Vulcan B.Mk.1 with the Phase 2 wing had indicated that, if full advantage was to be taken of the Olympus engine power potential, further changes to the outer wing would be required. This led to the new Phase 2C wing. Dimensions are shown overleaf.

During the first half of 1955, sufficient full-scale data was available to enable a submission to be made to the Ministry of Supply in August/September 1955 of a new wing planform design change to make full use of the anticipated development of the Olympus jet engine.

Design started on the B.Mk2 towards the end of 1955 under the guidance of Avro's chief designer, Roy Ewans. A prototype contract was placed in March 1956, followed in April 1956 by a production contract for the Vulcan B.Mk2 aircraft.

The new outer wings for the Mk2 were made and fitted to the existing second prototype Vulcan, VX777. This aircraft, in its modified form, had its first flight on 31 August 1957 followed by the first production aircraft in August 1958.

B.Mk2 contract review

Items listed in Ministry contact S.P.6/aircraft/11301/CB.6(a):

(a) Modified wing completed with control services
(b) Strengthened centre section
(c) Power flying controls to suit AC electrical system
(d) Strengthened main undercarriage
(e) Revision of de-icing system
(f) Revision of radio and radar cooling
(g) Pressurisation of radio and radar cooling
(h) Changes to emergency decompression system to suit increased rate of decompression at higher altitude
(i) Possible changes to operational equipment (supplied by Ministry of Supply) for operation at higher altitude
(j) Introduction of revised integrated auto-stabiliser equipment (yaw pitch and auto trimmer) superseding Modification No. 240
(k) Modified rudder and elevator artificial feel units (cast box type) incorporating failure warning
(l) Aileron artificial feel units incorporating failure warning
(m) Pressurised rudder power units
(n) Introduction of firewire resetting detector system for fuel tanks

Required amendments dated May 1957:

Installation of Olympus B.01.6 engine
Provision for high-thrust engines, etc
Introduction of new AC fuel pumps for high-thrust engines
Provision of electrical troughs to facilitate retrospective fitment of Mod 199
Introduction of autopilot Mk10A
Smiths military flight instrument system
Flight refuelling receiver version fixed fitting to cater for 1,000 GPM
Shortened nose undercarriage
Introduction of T.4 bomb site and associated equipment

Phase 2C wing dimensions

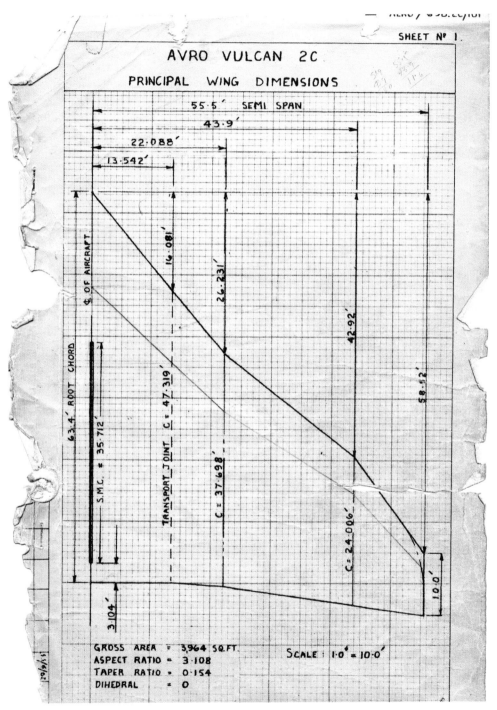

This data sheet, Aero/698.2C/101, was produced on 29 September 1955 and shows the principal wing dimensions for the Phase 2C wing. The new wing was thinner and larger than the Phase 2 kink wing designed for the B.Mk1/B.Mk1a.

The 1959 flight assessment

A pilot and engineering assessment report on the B.Mk2 was produced by Avro's chief test pilot, Jimmy Harrison, and C F Bethwaite, the chief flight development engineer, in 1959. The report summarised as briefly as possible the stage of development reached at the time of submitting the Vulcan B.Mk2 for preview trials at the Aeroplane and Armament Experimental Establishment (A&AEE). The first aircraft had completed approximately 40 hours of flying before preview but much of the development of the features that distinguish the B.Mk2 from the B.Mk1 aircraft had been carried out separately, using development aircraft VX777, XA893, XA891 and XA899 as flying test beds.

The report made no attempt to trace the various development troubles that had occurred on these test beds. Rather, attention was focused on the overall standard of the B.Mk2 in its present form. It was generally considered that the flying qualities of the Vulcan B.Mk2 fulfilled the design expectations and, even at the preview stage, there appeared to be only minor problems still to be investigated before full C(A) release trials. The general reliability of the aircraft was judged from the fact that the 30 hours up to the first minor inspection were completed in 29 days.

The aerodynamic prototype B.Mk2 (VX777), on 15 November 1957.

Brief summary of the flight assessment report

a) The change of wing aerodynamics had completely fulfilled the original predictions with regard to high Mach number buffet so that the increased thrust of the Olympus 200 series engines could be utilised as altitude performance without prejudice to the manoeuvrability of the aircraft.

b) The altitude performance was naturally superior to the B.Mk1 and it was interesting to record that the change of wing aerodynamics alone yielded a dividend of 2,000ft on the cruise ceiling of the aircraft. The additional engine thrust gave a further 4,000ft so that the target height of the B.Mk2 could be some 6,000ft in excess of the B.Mk1 figure at comparable weights. The possible inclusion of higher-thrust engines would increase this still further.

c) The handling qualities of the B.Mk2 were improved in several respects over those of the B.Mk1. In particular, both visibility and control on the approach was superior, and the aircraft had a high degree of manoeuvrability at cruising conditions.

d) The high Mach number characteristics of the basic aircraft were similar to those of the B.Mk1 and the static instability and loss of damping in pitch, which occurred well above cruising Mach number, were corrected by artificial stabilisation, similar to the B.Mk1 equipment but of improved design. This equipment had functioned extremely well so far.

e) The AC electrical system had so far given very little trouble and this was almost certainly due to the thorough test programmes carried out in flight on B.Mk1 aircraft and also on ground rigs.

Improvements could still be made to certain features. However, the time between A&AEE preview and C(A) release target would be adequate to carry out any further development necessary.

Conclusions

There were still one or two development aspects that had to be finalised before the Vulcan B.Mk2 was in a stage for submission for full C(A) release trials.

The major uncertainties at the time were concerned with the possible effects of the modified shape of the rear fuselage to accommodate the radio counter measures (RCM). It was generally felt that these effects would be small but, nevertheless, there might be unexpected changes in handling characteristics. These would be assessed when XH534 was flown.

Similarly, the aircraft had not yet been loaded to the maximum all-up weight, which would apply to the entry of the aircraft into service, and this could only be achieved after the inclusion of a number of structural modifications that had become necessary as a result of the progress on the structural specimen. The present programme scheduled the introduction of these modifications into XH534.

Other engineering improvements noted were the ability to support essential electrical loads from wind-milling engines to avoid the necessity for placing complete reliance upon the ram air turbine (RAT) should total flame-out occur. Simple and rapid engine starting, even without ground supplies, would make for easy worldwide operation and a high state of readiness. At best cruising Mach number for height and range, the aircraft was not dependant on artificial longitudinal stability. Success of the new wing in delaying the onset of buffet so that when cruising at the same weight but at much higher altitude than the B.Mk1, the buffet threshold was encountered at about 1.4g compared with 1.15g in the latest B.Mk1 with Olympus 104 engines. The docile take-off, approach and landing conditions would result in far lower break-off heights than the B.Mk1, which probably had the highest break-off height of any large aircraft in service.

Criticisms that might have been of concern to the A&AEE were that the high Mach number behaviour was unsatisfactory above .95 Indicated Mach Number (IMN) buffet and trim change due to high drag airbrakes at a high Mach number; excessive throttle friction; and the interference on intercom, especially with the instrument landing system (ILS) forward view in conditions of rain or external misting, was no better than that of the B.Mk1.

Mach trimmer installation

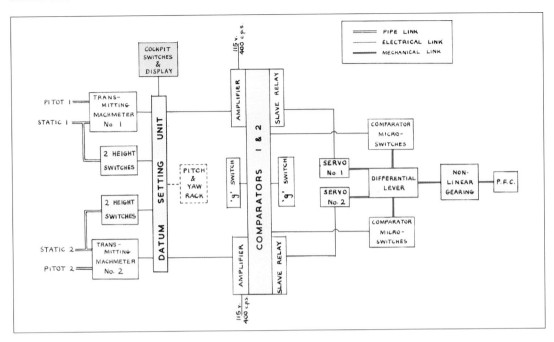

With a higher weight and improved performance of the Vulcan B.Mk2 required to achieve the same effective degree of stick-free stability as the B.Mk1, the total authority of the Mach trimmer in terms of movement of the trailing edge controls had to be increased. The system was altered to improve both the reliability and protection against malfunctioning and this was largely achieved by duplication of all components.

Avro Vulcan B.Mk1 (XA891), on 27 June 1956. It was the development aircraft for the Olympus B.016/35 jet engines, which were to be used on the B.Mk2. It crashed on 24 August 1959 due to total electrical failure.

New flying controls layout

A major change was to the flying control surfaces, from elevators and ailerons to elevons. The elevon control surfaces were operated independently by their own jacks and controlled from their own power unit, which was actuated by the common pilot's control on the input side. Failure of a power unit or jack would cause the corresponding section of the control surface to trail in the neutral position. The other three sections remain unaffected so that control of the aircraft at three-quarters of the full normal rate is then obtainable.

Conventional push-pull rods connected the control grips and rudder pedals to the power units. Artificial feel was provided to give a variation of stick force with control movement from the trimmed position. To give pleasant control forces and harmonisation over the speed range, the stick force rates are related to the response of the aircraft. An automatic stabilisation system was also incorporated.

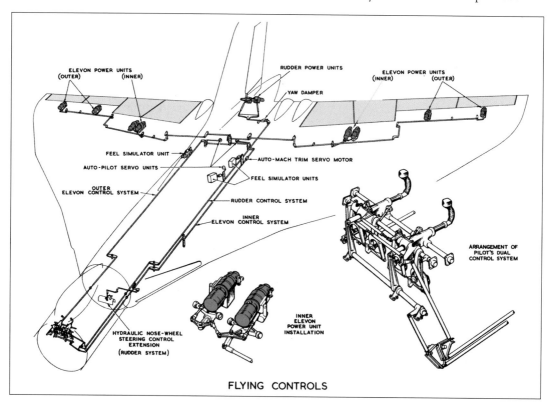

FLYING CONTROLS

Air brakes

Six efficient air brakes were situated in the centre section wing and extended above and below the aerofoil. They were actuated simultaneously by a centrally mounted actuator with duplicated electric motors controlled by a three-position lever in the cockpit. In the two extended positions the air brakes were used for three main purposes: to achieve high rates of descent without exceeding the speed limitations, to effect rapid deceleration from high air speeds and to give additional drag on the approach and landing.

Braking parachute

One 24ft-diameter ribbon parachute was installed on the starboard side of the tail fuselage below the rudder. It was provided primarily for use in emergency landings, such as a return to base soon after take-off. The position of the parachute installation changed when the new rear fuselage ECM was fitted.

New electrical system

The 112-volt DC electrical system of the Vulcan B.Mk1 and B.Mk1a aircraft was replaced in its entirety by a four-channel, three-phase 200-volt, 400-cycle-per-second (cps) alternating current (AC) system. This was of significant importance in that the Vulcan B.Mk2 was the first aircraft in the UK to be fitted with such a system.

The system design specification, AE7510, for this three-phase system was proposed by the Aircraft Equipment Division, Special Products Group of the English Electric Co. Ltd, Bradford, and was accepted and incorporated into the Vulcan B.Mk2 aircraft by Mr P C 'Paddy' Finucane, the chief electrical design engineer at Avro Chadderton.

The system comprised four 40kVA AC generators, each driven via a hydro-mechanical constant speed drive (CSD) from an aircraft engine. The output voltage of the AC generator was controlled at 200 volts plus or minus 5-volt RMS by a carbon pile-type voltage regulator and the frequency by a frequency and load controller acting on the output speed of the CSD to control the output of the AC generator at 400 plus or minus 4cps.

Power supplies are used for the following services:

200-volt, three-phase	Flying controls, fuel pumps and their controls, 400-cycle AC air brakes, radar, emergency hydraulic power (alternators) pack and instruments
115-volt, 400-cycle	Radar, controls for cabin atmosphere, bomb bay AC heating, anti-icing, and lighting and instruments
115-volt, 1600-cycle	Radar
28-volt DC	Instruments, warning lights, radio, bomb gear, lighting and controls for alternators, secondary power supplies and electro-hydraulic equipment
28-volt DC (batteries)	Vital service, i.e., crash and fire and starting (batteries) for the auxiliary power unit

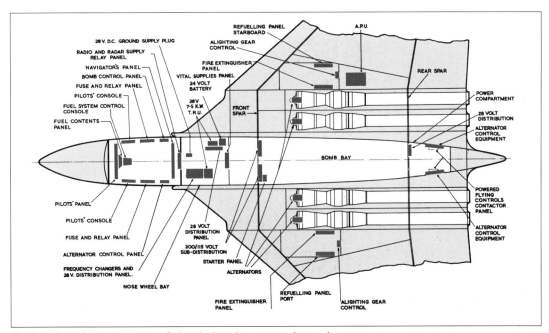

The locations of the main items of electrical equipment are shown above.

The AC generators were each connected to a separate busbar to which the electrical loads were connected via three phase contactors and also via similar contactors to a common synchronising busbar.

All 200-volt AC services use three-phase wiring from a star-connected supply, the neutral being brought out for use with MERZ PRICE protection. All 28-volt DC services use single pole wiring, the negative return being taken through the airframe. An extensive voltage regulation and alternator protection system was provided and all services were protected by fuses and, in some cases, by circuit breakers. Two international ground supply plugs were installed on the port side of the fuselage, one for 200 volts AC and the other for 28 volts DC.

Normal operation was to synchronise the generators of channel 1 and channel 4 via the synchronising busbar, connect the channel 2 generator automatically via a synchronising monitor unit to the synchronising busbar (if it was de-energised), and to run the channel 3 generator connected in isolation to its own load busbar, in case of a synchronising busbar failure.

It was also possible to select each generator to only supply its own load busbar or to parallel any of the generators or all in a four-channel paralleled operation, although in practice this was not done.

If the synchronising busbar is de-energised in flight sufficient powered flying control units are energised to enable control of the aircraft to be maintained, via the synchronising busbar, from the RAT from altitudes of 60,000–20,000ft. This requires the pilot to maintain between 0.95 and 0.85 Mach, i.e., 365–250 knots to maintain a generator frequency of 380–420cps while descending to an altitude of less than 30,000ft where the airborne auxiliary power pack could be started to take over the electrical loads from the RAT.

On the ground, all loads were supplied via the synchronising busbar from a ground power unit.

Interlocking and voltage monitoring ensured that only one of these sources could be connected to the synchronising busbar at any one time.

Generator output circuit protection for all four main generators was provided against over-voltage, under-voltage, incorrect phase sequence, and differential currents from the AC generator exceeding 40 amps.

The real loads (kW) and the reactive loads (kVAR) of paralleled generators were controlled by load-sharing loops on each channel to plus and minus 5kw and 5kvars of the mean loads of the paralleled machines.

The consumer loads of each generator were protected by fuses or circuit breakers.

A 115-volt 400-cycle AC was provided from two step-down transformers from the 200-volt supplies.

A 115-volt 1600-cycle AC was provided from three frequency changers also from the 200-volt supply.

Direct current power at 28 volts was provided from two 7.5kw transformer rectifier units, and a single 28-volt 40-ampere-hour nickel cadmium battery provided sufficient power for crash and emergency services.

The control and monitoring of the electrical systems was carried out by the air electronics officer (AEO) from the panel on the port wall of the pressure cabin at the rear operator's position.

Development

Before the 200-volt 400cps system was installed in the aircraft, the full electrical system was assembled in the Electrical Development Department laboratory at Avro Chadderton. The Olympus engines were replicated by four 500-volt DC 120-horsepower machines, with control equipment to enable the speed variations and rates of change of acceleration – from start-up to take-off speeds of the engine – to be reproduced.

Artificial electrical loading from resistors and inductive chokes allowed loads at various power factors to be selected. Means were provided to test each of the protection circuits for correct operation in accordance with the specification limits. Endurance testing, initially up to 500 hours' duration, was also carried out.

The carbon pile voltage regulators required a 20-minute pile warm-up time before the voltage could be set to the limits. This was overcome by the introduction of the solid-state silicon-controlled regulator (SCR) when the appropriate semiconductors became available. The design of the SCR voltage regulator was the brainchild of Dr H Lathom, the electrical design engineer at Avro Chadderton and liaison with English Electric Bradford for its manufacture as AE7306.

At high altitude, the commutator carbon brushes of the alternator were quickly worn away due to lack of atmospheric lubrication at such a height.

Initially, molybdenum disulphide cores were inserted in the carbon brushes, which decreased the rate of wear, but brushless AC generators were the only complete solution, and they were introduced at a later date.

The extensive laboratory testing of the individual components prior to being fitted to the aircraft, the testing of the complete aircraft system up to full loads of 40kVA at power factors up to 0.8 and the testing of the protection circuits ensured safe operation in service.

The laboratory shown here was used for testing the Nimrod electrical system, which was previously used for testing the Vulcan's electrical system at Chadderton.

The control console for the electrical systems and DC prime movers.

The laboratory machine room at Woodford with four prime mover 60kVA alternators on the left gear-box output positions and a 40kVA Vulcan CSD/Alt connected to the right gear-box output position. The alternator is shown coupled by a flexible hose.

Additional safety features

An early issue that concerned the electrics was the running of the carbon pile voltage regulators, which required a 20-minute warming time before the alternator voltage could be set to 115 ± 5 phase to neutral to allow correct load sharing when paralleled. These were subsequently replaced by SCR static regulators, which were set up during manufacture to the correct voltage and eliminated the need for pre-flight adjustment.

In the event of failure of the aircraft alternators, a RAT, which comprised a mechanically governed, air-driven turbine assembly coupled to a 22kVA alternator was fitted to the Vulcan. The unit was mounted on a platform and lowered into the airstream. Once lowered, the RAT could not be retracted back into the fuselage. Development work on the RAT was carried out on XH560.

Ram air turbine (RAT)

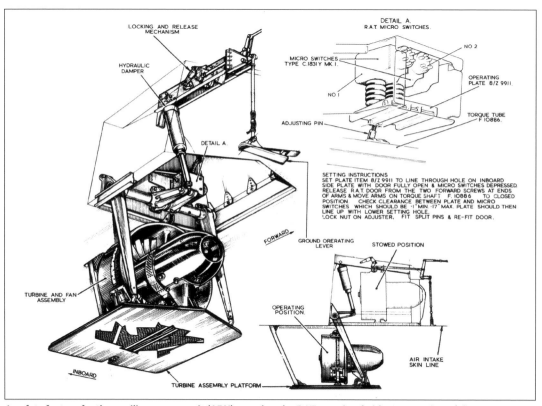

A safety feature for the auxiliary power unit (APU) was that the RAT permitted airborne starting of the Rover gas turbine.

Airborne auxiliary power unit (APU)

The airborne APU comprised a Rover gas turbine engine driving a 40kVA AC generator through a train of gears. A supply of compressed air could also be bled off. The engine was a single-sided centrifugal compressor driven by a single-stage axial turbine mounted on a common shaft and supported on two bearings.

Limits on a typical flight performance were 23kW for a period not exceeding four minutes, 0 to 5,000ft with undercarriage down, 13kW for periods up to 30 minutes, 0 to 10,000ft at 130–415 EAS and 17kW for periods up to 30 minutes, 10,000 to 30,000ft at 185–415kt or Mach 0.95 (whichever was less).

Changes to radar and radio equipment

The new ECM that was fitted to the B.Mk1A Vulcan was not included in the initial B.Mk2 brochure.

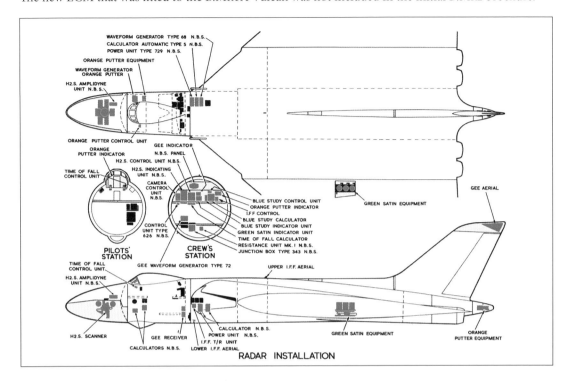

RADAR INSTALLATION

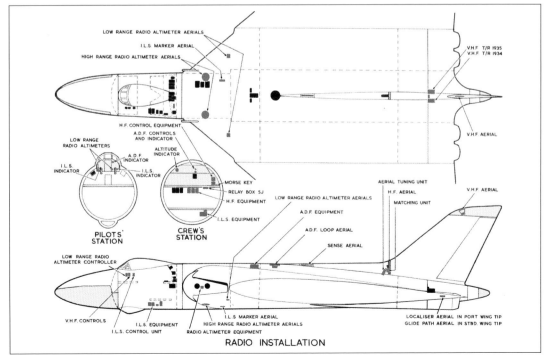

RADIO INSTALLATION

Radar and radio

The radar and radio equipment were more or less similar to B.Mk1 Vulcan's, which included bombing, navigational and landing aids, tail warning equipment and an identification, friend or foe (IFF) installation.

The additional bombing aid, known as Blue Study, was provided by equipment that controlled the aircraft automatically on a defined track.

Tail warning radar, which indicated the range and direction of fighters approaching from the rear, was installed as a complete unit in the tail fairing of the fuselage. The equipment, known as Orange Putter and later Red Steer, was controlled from the signaller's station and indicators were provided for the signaller and the pilots.

A Marconi AD 7092 D radio compass was installed with a master indicator and controls at the master navigator's station. Repeaters were fitted to both pilots' panels. The receiver was mounted above the No. 2 tank bay and the loop and its drive mechanism in the roof of the bomb bay. A sense aerial was built into the forward end of the dorsal fin and immediately aft of the radio compass.

Fuel system

The number of wing fuel tanks and capacities remained the same as the B.Mk1. Included was the option of bomb bay fuel tanks as illustrated below. The 14 bag-type fuel tanks were contained in magnesium-alloy compartments. The control of the fuel supply was arranged so that the balance of the aircraft was maintained between the desired limits.

The aircraft could also be equipped either as a receiver or a tanker, using the well-known probe-and-drogue system. The total fuel weight quoted for a 10,000lb bomb load was 4,358lb and 4,512lb with the special 13,000lb store.

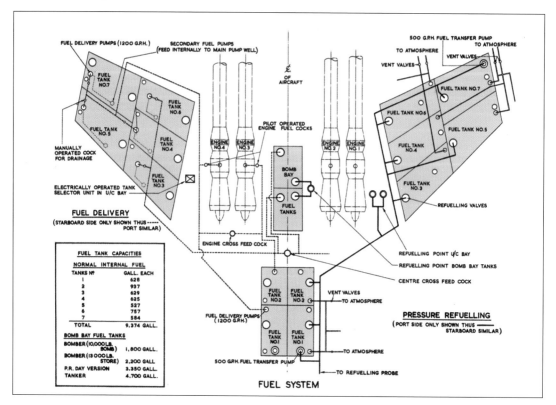

FUEL SYSTEM

FUEL TANK CAPACITIES	
NORMAL INTERNAL FUEL	
TANKS Nº	**GALL. EACH**
1	626
2	937
3	629
4	625
5	527
6	757
7	584
TOTAL	9,374 GALL.
BOMB BAY FUEL TANKS	
BOMBER (10,000LB. BOMB)	1,800 GALL.
BOMBER (13,000LB. STORE)	2,200 GALL
P.R. DAY VERSION	3,350 GALL.
TANKER	4,700 GALL.

Leading particulars

General dimensions	
Length overall	97ft 1in
Span overall	111ft
Height	26ft 6in
Mainplane data	
Chord at centreline	63.40ft
Chord at tip	10ft
Chord mean	35.71ft
Aerofoil section at wing joint NACA 0010	
Thickness chord ratio	10 per cent
Aerofoil section at wing tip RAE.101 modified	
Thickness chord ratio	5 per cent
Incidence	5 degrees
Dihedral	0 degrees
Aspect ratio	3.11
Sweepback (leading edge at wing joint)	49 deg. 54 min

Fin and rudder data	
Sweepback (leading edge)	49 deg. 30 min
Thickness chord ratio	10 per cent
Wing area (in square feet)	
Gross	3,964
Elevons (inner)	241.78
Elevons (outer)	109.73
(aft of hinge line)	
Areas (in square feet)	
Fin and rudder	325
Fin (nett)	160
Rudder (aft of hinge line)	63.4
Hydraulic system	
Working pressure	3,600lb/sq in
Off load pressure	4,000lb/sq in
Reservoir capacity	2¼ gal
System capacity	12 gal
Pneumatic system	
Charging pressure	2000lb/sq in
Total capacity (2 cylinders)	1,666 litres

Internal arrangement – March 1956

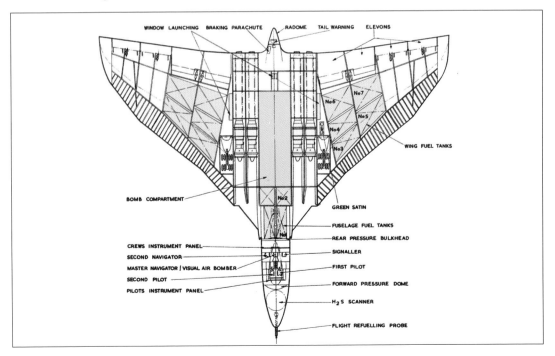

Development with Blue Steel

In November 1956, a brochure was produced outlining a series of further development of the B.Mk2 Vulcan.

The largest engines at that time, proposed by either Rolls-Royce or Bristol, could be installed in later B.Mk2 aircraft, which would have enlarged intakes to accommodate the greater mass flows involved.

Introduction

In addition to the proposals for the outer wing changes laid down in the Vulcan Phase 2C (Brochure IPB62) a number of internal changes had been made to the aircraft. The most important of these was provision for the installation of the Avro Blue Steel weapon, together with RCM equipment and extra fuel tanks in the bomb bay, the installation of more powerful engines – initially the Rolls-Royce Conway 11 at 16,500lb SLST or the Bristol Olympus 6 at 16,000lb SLST with the possibility of later development to the Conway 31 or Olympus 21 stage 3 ratings.

Wind-tunnel tests made in the high-speed tunnel at the RAE confirmed the aerodynamic characteristics predicted for the Mk2 Vulcan and it was now possible to contemplate further aerodynamic refinements to make it possible to cruise at higher lift coefficients and consequently to use engines of 19,000–20,000lb SLST, namely the Bristol Olympus 21 stage 3 and the Rolls-Royce Conway 31, with a consequent valuable increase in altitude.

Design studies of the installation of these engines had, therefore, been made. In this connection it should be remembered that the carriage of Blue Steel externally increased the drag of the aircraft and the cruising lift coefficient was therefore reduced for the same engine power.

Enlarged engine air intakes

To achieve maximum efficiency from these engines, which had a much greater air mass flow even than those that were foreseen for the Vulcan, it was found necessary to increase the size of the air intakes. The larger intakes had been accommodated without any major alterations to other components of the aircraft. The upper wing surface and top intake lips remained unaltered, but the lower wing surface, forward of the front spar, was revised to achieve the greater intake cross-sectional area, while retaining a bottom lip of similar shape to the present intake. These shapes of lips had been retained because their behaviour was known to be satisfactory throughout the speed range of the aircraft and no development difficulties were, therefore, anticipated with the larger intakes. The existing airbrake legs, which straddled the intakes remained unaltered and cleared the larger ducts. The enlarged air intake would not be incorporated in the first few B.Mk2 aircraft and was therefore only suitable for the Conway 11 at 16,500lb SLST or the Olympus series up to 17,500lb.

Integration of bomb bay equipment

To develop the concept of a weapon system for the Vulcan, the arrangement of the various stores together with other equipment located in the bomb bay was co-ordinated to achieve maximum interchange ability, compatible with efficiency.

The three main items to be carried were:
 (a) the store, i.e. Blue Danube, Blue Steel, Yellow Sun or Red Beard
 (b) RCM installation, including the glycol-cooling system
 (c) extra-long-range internal fuel tanks located in the bomb bay

With the exception of Blue Steel. all the other stores mentioned above were stowed internally within the bomb bay. It had been found possible to design the RCM installation in such a manner that it was similar for all stores but, to achieve maximum range, the extra fuel tanks for Blue Steel were different from those required for the Blue Danube and Yellow Sun installations.

Blue Steel installation with RCM and bomb bay fuel

The installation of the Blue Steel store was not totally enclosed within the bomb bay, but rather half-submerged. This necessitated the replacing of the existing bomb doors by a fixed fairing, extending in the fore and aft direction from the front to rear spar and in the lateral direction across the bomb bay. This fairing was dished to accommodate the upper surface of the Blue Steel missile. The bottom boom of the front spar had been cranked to pass over the top of the nose of the missile. Minor modifications were required to the aircraft structure forward of the front spar and small changes were made to the fuel tanks in that region. Inside the bomb bay, the RCM installation was similar to that used with the Blue Danube and Yellow Sun stores, but considerably more space was available for fuel, and consequently two tanks of larger capacity were designed to carry some 2,450 gallons. All B.Mk2 aircraft were given the modifications necessary to carry Blue Steel.

Aircraft drag

The drag of the Vulcan B.Mk2 was based directly on the comprehensive drag measurements made by A V Roe and A&AEE on the present series of Vulcan B.Mk1 aircraft. Confirmation of these results had also been obtained from Bomber Command after a series of long flights made under strictly controlled cruise conditions. Preliminary confirmation of the basic B.Mk2 aircraft drag had been obtained from the tests being made in the RAE high-speed wind tunnel. These tests also confirmed that the compressibility drag rise was delayed to a considerably higher Mach number than on the B.Mk1 aircraft, probably due to the thinner outer wing. The results were modified for the new wing planform of the B.Mk2 aircraft and for the carriage of the Blue Steel missile. The additional drag due to Blue Steel was based on the high-speed tunnel tests reported in RAE/TN/Aero/2365.

B.Mk2 Summary

Both the second prototype in its Mk.2 configuration and the first production aircraft were used for the handling and performance trials. As indicated earlier, some B.Mk1 aircraft were used for system developments for the production B.Mk.2 aircraft. These systems covered engine installations (Bristol Olympus B.01.6) and the AC electrical system.

The second B.Mk2 production aircraft was used to carry out the official A&AEE trials during the early part of 1960.

The initial C(A) release for the Vulcan B.Mk2 was issued by the Ministry of Supply in May 1960. The delivery of the first Mk2 aircraft (XH558) took place the following month.

B.Mk2 development aircraft

As with the B.Mk.1 aircraft, some early B.Mk2 production aircraft were used to clear the Vulcan B.Mk2:
Vulcan B.Mk2 (VX777) handling and development
Vulcan B.Mk1 (XA893) AC electrical system
Vulcan B.Mk1 (XA899) Mk10A autopilot and military flight system (MFS)
Vulcan B.Mk1 (XA891) BOL.06 engine development
Vulcan B.Mk2 (XH533) handling and performance
Vulcan B.Mk2 (XH534) A&AEE release trials
Vulcan B.Mk2 (XH535) final conference
Vulcan B.Mk2 (XH536) radio and radar
Vulcan B.Mk2 (XH537) armament
Vulcan B.Mk2 (XH538) Blue Steel
Vulcan B.Mk2 (XH557) enlarged intake, bomb bay fuel tanks, increase in gross weight
Vulcan B.Mk1 (XA895) RCM development
Vulcan B.Mk2 (XA558) RCM service trials (first aircraft to enter RAF service)

Post-C(A) release

Further developments to the B.Mk2 took place on later production aircraft, covering electronic equipment, the Blue Steel stand-off weapon and the introduction of the Olympus B.01.21 engine.

A major development was the proposed introduction of the United States airborne ballistic missile 'Skybolt'. An intensive development programme was carried out in close collaboration with the Douglas Aircraft Corporation up to the time (December 1962) when this weapon was abandoned as a result of government policy decisions.

The first production B.Mk2, XH533, on 31 August 1958, the day after its first flight. The aircraft was used for handling, performance and automatic landing trials.

B.Mk2 Production

An order was placed for 37 B.Mk1 aircraft in September 1954. There were two amendments to this order: the first, in April 1956, was for 30 B.Mk1s and seven B.Mk2s; the second, in June 1957, was for 20 B.Mk1s and 17 B.Mk2s. A contract for eight B.Mk1 aircraft, placed on 31 March 1955, was amended to eight B.Mk2 aircraft on 1 June 1956, and a contract for 24 B.Mk1s, placed on 26 February 1956, was amended on 1 June to B.Mk2s. A final contract was issued for 40 B.Mk2s, placed on 22 January 1958. The total number built, including prototypes, was 136.

B.Mk2 contracts

B.Mk2	17 aircraft	XH533–XH563	Sets 1–25
B.Mk2	8 aircraft	XJ780–XJ825	Sets 26–49
B.Mk2	24 aircraft	XL317–XL446	Sets 50–67
B.Mk2	40 aircraft	XM596–XM657	Sets 68–89

Batch numbers			Production Set No.
B.Mk2 Batch 5	25 aircraft	XH533–XJ825	Sets 46–70
B.Mk2 Batch 6	24 aircraft	XL317–XL446	Sets 71–94
B.Mk2 Batch 7	18 aircraft	XM569–XM603	Sets 95–112
		XM596	Set 60 FTS
B.Mk2 Batch 8	22 aircraft	XM604–XM657	Sets 113–134

The last aircraft to be delivered was XM657 (set number 89), which made its first flight on 21 December 1964 and was delivered on 14 January 1965.

Significant milestones

Vulcan Mk2 proposed	August 1955
Wing leading edge modification designed	September 1955
Leading edge modification fitted (VX777)	October 1955
Vulcan Mk2 prototype contract	March 1956
First flight of Vulcan Mk.2 (VX777)	August 1957
Vulcan Mk2 ECM proposed	May 1958
First flight of production Vulcan Mk2 (XH533)	August 1958
Vulcan Mk2 C(A) release	May 1960
Vulcan Mk2 to squadron (XH558)	July 1960
Vulcan Mk2 with ECM fitted	November 1960
First production Mk2 Vulcan modified for Blue Steel (XL317)	June 1961
First production B.Mk2 with Olympus 301 engines (XJ784)	August 1961
First Mk2 converted to carry Skybolt	September 1961

The assembly line at Woodford and nose
assembly at Chadderton (inset).

New ECM Equipment

In May 1958, it was first proposed to fit the B.Mk2 with a new ECM suite and radar in an enlarged rear fuselage. The second production aircraft, XH534, was the first B.Mk2 to be fitted with this equipment.

The transmitters and power units were in large pressurised 'cans' and could get quite hot when in operation; these cans were kept cool by vapour cycle heat exchangers. On the starboard side of the ECM compartment, an air intake provided cooling air. Electrical power for the ECM was provided by a bleed air turbine (BAT) powered by air taken from No. 3 or No. 4 engine and drove a 200-volt three-phase alternator. This was necessary because the B.Mk1 had a 112-volt DC electrical system. The BAT was not needed on the B.Mk2, with its 200-volt AC system, and its position, just aft of the starboard main wheel bay, was filled by a Rover gas-turbine-powered APU.

All ECMs were controlled by the AEO. During one of the ECM test flights, a full test was made of the equipment, which led to the black-out of all radio and TV transmissions in the vicinity of the Vulcan. From that day onwards, Cabinet approval had to be obtained before testing of the equipment could be carried out.

The Red Steer tail warning radar was situated in the rear tip of the compartment and the brake parachute relocated under a hatch just to the rear of the rudder.

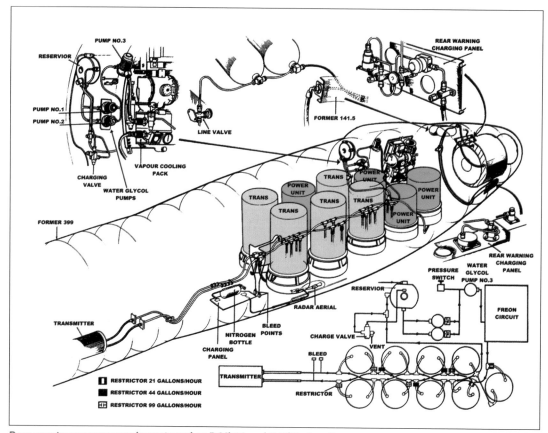

Rear counter measures equipment used on B.Mk1A and B.Mk2 aircraft.

Above left and above right: Canister heat exchangers on a test rig in final form, April 1963.

ECM equipment

ARI 18105
Blue Saga radar-warning receiver

ARI 18074
Green Palm – voice communications jammer

ARI 18075
Blue Diver – (airborne radio installation)
low-band VHF jammer replaced Green Palm

ARI 18076
Red Shrimp – airborne high-band jammer

A.R.I. 18105 REAR FUSELAGE EQUIPMENT

XH534 was the first B.Mk2 to be fitted with the new counter measures suite.

Ultimate Power

The final engines used on the Vulcan were the Olympus 201 and 301 versions. The Olympus 301 was designated the Olympus B.01.21A.

The Olympus 200 started life under the designation B.01.6, which produced 16,000lb of thrust. It first ran at Patchway, Bristol, in September 1954. Later, a developed version, the B.01.7, produced 17,000lb of thrust. In May 1958, B.01.7 had completed its test programme and was fitted to XA891 for further work at both Filton and Woodford.

The first Olympus 200 engine flew in the first production Vulcan B.Mk2 (XH533) on 19 August 1958. In 1959 the second B.Mk2 (XH534) was equipped with Olympus 201 engines of 17,000lb thrust and used for A&AEE trials.

When the series 201 entered service, it was to encounter problems of engine surging, mainly with the inboard engine at medium- to high-altitude; this led to attempts by Avro to improve the airflow at the intake. The aircraft used for these trials was XH560, which had returned to Woodford on 23 December 1960 and was later allotted for Skybolt development on 29 May 1961. The surge problem was finally solved by cut-back of the LP turbine stators by 2 per cent and that, combined with a revised fuel system schedule, resulted in surge-free handling.

With the requirement for more thrust, a new Olympus was designed to give an increase in thrust of 20,000lb. These changes were made so that a 201 could easily be converted to the new standard and bore the type number B.01.21A. The new engine first ran at Patchway in January 1959. With the increase in thrust, Avro designed intakes to accept the larger capacity of the new engine. By this time Bristol had merged with Armstrong Siddeley Engines in 1959 and became known as Bristol Siddeley Engines Limited (BSEL).

Vulcan XH557 had been allotted to BSEL for the new engine installation. So that the larger B.01.21A could replace the 201 Olympus engines on XH557, structural alterations had to be made to the airframe. XH557 flew for the first time with the new engine on 19 May 1961 and was then delivered to Woodford for handling assessment trials. Later, 301 engines were used for handling, calibration and engine performance. The Olympus 301 was not a trouble-free engine: as with the 201 the engine, it was to encounter surge problems on the inboard engine. This led to a raising of the idle speed by 10 per cent to help solve the problem. However, engine surging was to plague the 301 version of the Olympus throughout its career. Avro had fitted intake vortex generators to XJ784 in an attempt to improve

inboard engine handling; a slight improvement was observed but not enough to justify service use. At high altitude, oil loss was also experienced with the rear turbine bearing. Various alterations were tried before a final solution was found. Avro converted XJ784 to accept four Olympus 301 engines and the aircraft went to A&AEE in April 1962 for initial C(A) release trials. Following a limited clearance, the 301 finally entered service with the RAF in June 1963.

Another problem experienced by the Vulcan, especially in its day-time role, was the smoke trail that could be seen from some distance. A series of service trials were held in 1971 and 1972. This involved the changing of the core angle of the fuel spray. The first trial took place on XH558 and the smoke trail was effectively reduced but with engine-handling problems. A second trial on XL392 found that inadequate smoke reduction had occurred for the modification to be accepted for service use. A final trial on Olympus 202 engines achieved a compromise between handling and smoke emission, and this version was accepted for service use; all 201s/202s in service were modified. In August 1975, XM648 with modified burners on two 301 engines was used to help eliminate the smoke trail issue, but this was not without handling problems and this version was not taken forward due to the expense and limited life of the Vulcan in service.

The engine surge problems were due, in part, to the common air intake and disturbance to air on the inboard engine. For the Olympus 301 engine, XJ784 was used for vortex generator testing. The vortex generators were placed inboard the air intake; a slight improvement was noticed. It can be seen here, above right, during airflow test, with the boundary layer extended without vortex generators. The larger intake on XH554, shown above (right), was designed for the more powerful Olympus engines. Also shown is the boundary splitter used to ensure the entry of undisturbed high-speed air to help increase the maximum flow rate of air into the engine.

One of the noticeable airframe differences between Olympus series 200 and 300 engines was that the tail pipe shroud of the 200 series was longer, narrower and more tapered than the Olympus 301 series engine.

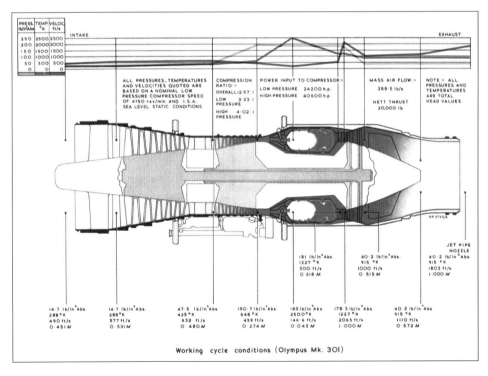

Working cycle conditions (Olympus Mk. 301)

It is worth noting that in 1959 it was announced that Avro was to enter the civil market with the Avro 748 turboprop feeder airliner. This was due to the slowdown in military work and the lack of new military projects. This, combined with military defence cuts, led to the Vulcan being the only viable long-range nuclear bomber available to the RAF in the mid-1970s.

For the Vulcan to be a reliable weapons system, it was continuously updated to meet the different roles that it was assigned, which kept the innovative Avro Initial Projects Department team busy for more than two decades.

As can be seen from the chart below, most of the major developments had been completed by 1962–63 with the introduction of the B.Mk2 into service.

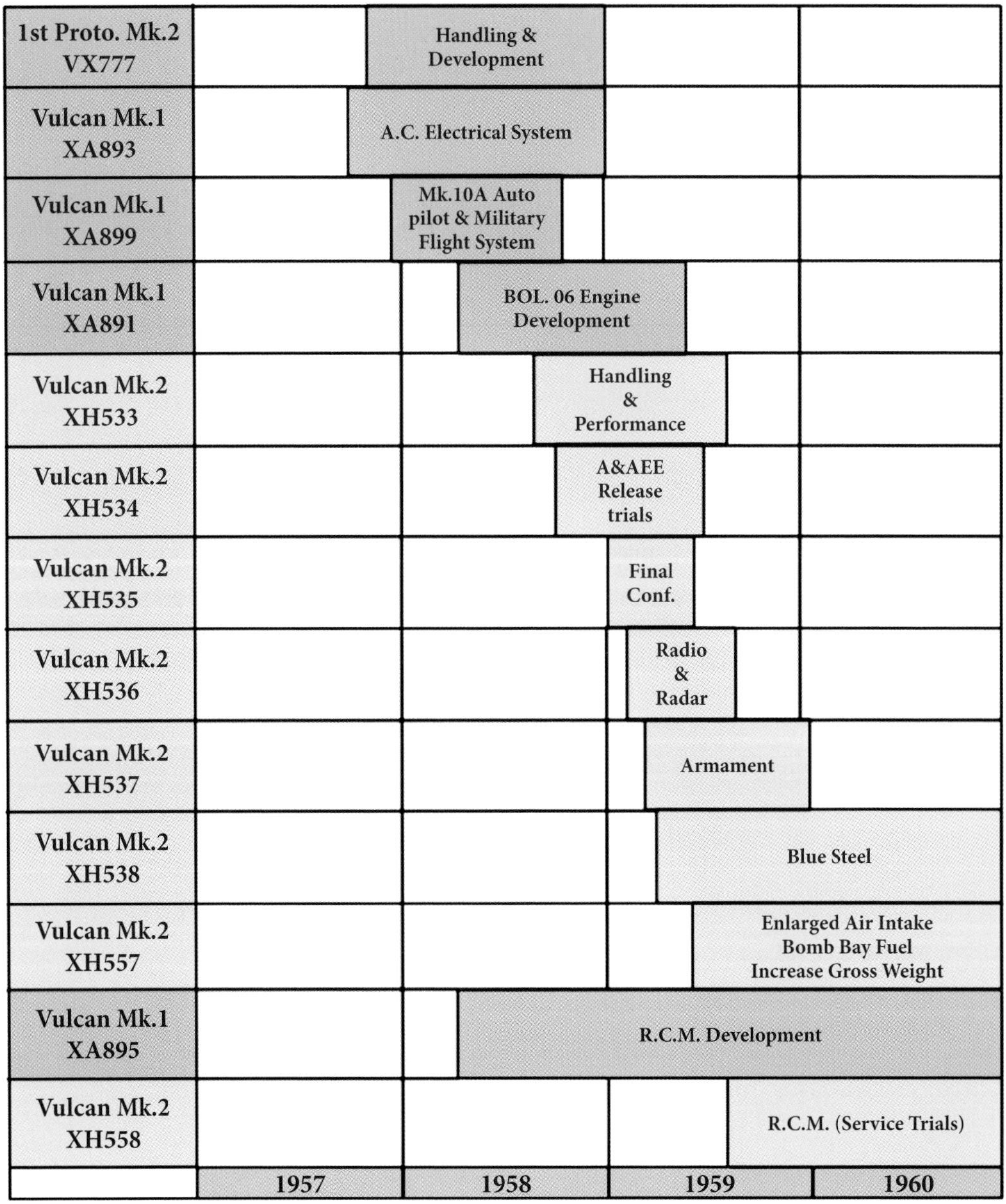

	1957	1958	1959	1960
1st Proto. Mk.2 VX777		Handling & Development		
Vulcan Mk.1 XA893		A.C. Electrical System		
Vulcan Mk.1 XA899		Mk.10A Auto pilot & Military Flight System		
Vulcan Mk.1 XA891		BOL. 06 Engine Development		
Vulcan Mk.2 XH533			Handling & Performance	
Vulcan Mk.2 XH534			A&AEE Release trials	
Vulcan Mk.2 XH535			Final Conf.	
Vulcan Mk.2 XH536			Radio & Radar	
Vulcan Mk.2 XH537			Armament	
Vulcan Mk.2 XH538				Blue Steel
Vulcan Mk.2 XH557				Enlarged Air Intake Bomb Bay Fuel Increase Gross Weight
Vulcan Mk.1 XA895			R.C.M. Development	
Vulcan Mk.2 XH558				R.C.M. (Service Trials)

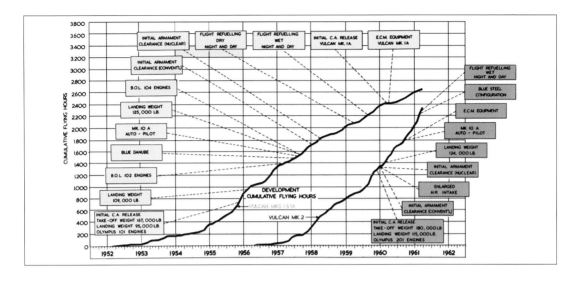

Vulcan B.Mk2 all-up weights of bombing cases

Blue Steel	
Operational weight – 5 crew	108,904lb
Removable bomb gear	1,495lb
Store	15,700lb
Rapid blooming window	480lb
100 per cent normal fuel 9,400 gal @ SG 0.77	72,380lb
Total take-off weight	199,009lb
Landing with store, window and 10,000lb fuel	136,629lb
Maximum take-off weight with bay fuel tanks	211,510lb

7000lb MC Yellow Sun	
Operational weight – 5 crew	108,904lb
Removable bomb gear	295lb
Store	7,200lb
Rapid blooming window	480lb
100 per cent normal fuel 9,400 gal @ SG 0.77	72,380lb
Total take-off weight	189,259lb
Landing with store, window and 10,000lb fuel	126,879lb
Maximum take-off weight with bay fuel tanks	198,206lb

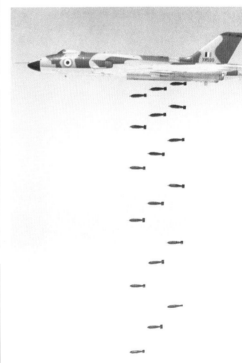

21 x 1000lb store	
Operational weight – 5 crew	108,904lb
Removable bomb gear	762lb
Store	21,000lb
Rapid blooming window	480lb
100 per cent normal fuel 9,400 gal @ SG 0.77	72,380lb
Total take-off weight	203,526lb
Landing with store, window and 10,000lb fuel	141,146lb

Blue Steel Initial Development

Advances in the defence of the V-bomber's main targets led the Air Ministry to look at stand-off weapons for the aircraft, to increase its value as a deterrent and its chances of survival.

Working to operational requirement OR1132, issued by the Ministry of Supply on 3 September 1954, Avro formed a weapons research division in 1954, based at Woodford, to design a stand-off missile to meet this operational requirement. It was headed by Hugh Francis, who came from the RAE at Farnborough. Also employed was John Allen, who had supervised the

Early 19/15 test model.

ballistics and aircraft integration of Blue Danube at Farnborough. He was the deputy chief engineer at the weapons research division at Avro and instrumental in the design of Blue Steel.

In February 1957, the Avro Weapons Research Division had chosen a site at Edinburgh Field, Salisbury, in Australia, which was about 16 miles north of Adelaide and about 250 miles south from the test range at Woomera. The site was chosen for live testing of the new missile being built at Chadderton and Woodford. Trials began in August 1957 with two-fifths scale un-powered models being dropped from a Vickers Valiant; a scale powered model flew in February 1958. Vulcan B.Mk1 XA903 was allotted in May 1957 to carry the full-scale version and arrived at Edinburgh airfield on 16 November 1960. By this time, the missile was publicly known as the 'Blue Steel' stand-off missile.

The Blue Steel trials team arrived in July 1957 and started missile testing scale models in August 1957 with Valiant aircraft. In 1960, No. 4 Joint Services Trials Unit (No. 4 JSTU) arrived in Australia and started testing the full-scale version of the Blue Steel missile.

Development flights started in Australia, with round ten in 1961 with the Vickers Valiant. The first attempted launch from a Vulcan B.Mk2 XH539 was on 23 March 1962, with the first successful launch on 2 July 1962. On 4 October 1962, Victor XL161 successfully launched round 60. Many overflights were also conducted using a live missile testing system, i.e. Green Satin, autopilot, APU etc. One flight at high level covered a long range of 160 miles. On 19 November 1963 a low-level launch was made by Avro Vulcan B.Mk2 XH539. High-level launches were conducted between 48,000 and 56,000ft; low-level launches were below 1,000ft, with 25 being successful.

In 1962 a report was produced by the A&AEE at Boscombe Down on the carriage and release of the B.Mk2 converted to the Blue Steel role. These trials were completed between November 1961 and January 1962. The Type 100A Blue Steel missile was used for the majority of the flight trials. Subject to the incorporation of modifications detailed in the report, the missile was deemed suitable for service use. The functioning of the missile was the subject of separate trials in Australia.

Valiants based at Woodford were used in the test programme.

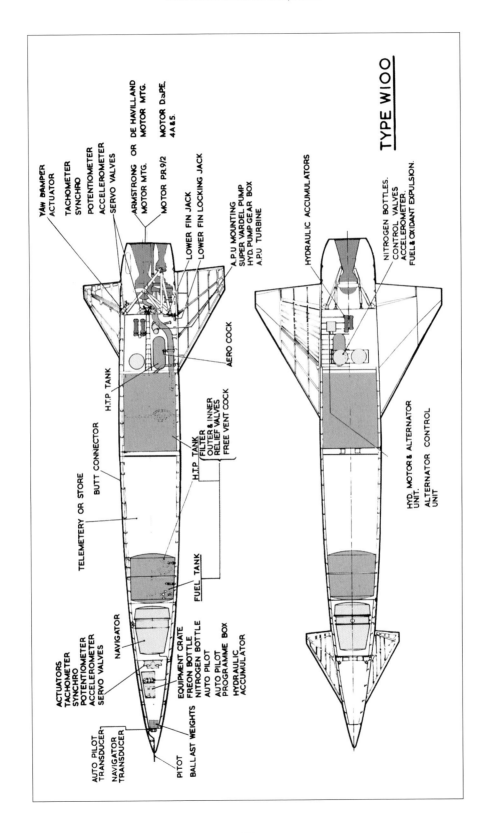

TYPE W100

YAW DAMPER ACTUATOR
TACHOMETER SYNCHRO
POTENTIOMETER
ACCELEROMETER
SERVO VALVES
ARMSTRONG OR DE HAVILLAND MOTOR MTG.
MOTOR MTG.
MOTOR PR.9/2
MOTOR D.s.P.E. 4A&5.
LOWER FIN JACK
LOWER FIN LOCKING JACK
A.P.U MOUNTING
SUPER VARDEL PUMP
HYD. PUMP GEAR BOX
A.P.U TURBINE
AERO COCK
HYDRAULIC ACCUMULATORS
NITROGEN BOTTLES.
CONTROL VALVES
ACCELEROMETER.
FUEL & OXIDANT EXPULSION.

ACTUATORS
TACHOMETER
SYNCHRO
POTENTIOMETER
ACCELEROMETER
SERVO VALVES
NAVIGATOR
TELEMETERY OR STORE
BUTT CONNECTOR
H.T.P TANK
H.T.P TANK
FILTER
OUTER & INNER RELIEF VALVES
FREE VENT COCK
FUEL TANK
EQUIPMENT CRATE
FREON BOTTLE
NITROGEN BOTTLE
AUTO PILOT
AUTO PILOT PROGRAMME BOX
HYDRAULIC ACCUMULATOR
AUTO PILOT TRANSDUCER
NAVIGATOR TRANSDUCER
PITOT
BALLAST WEIGHTS

HYD. MOTOR & ALTERNATOR UNIT.
ALTERNATOR CONTROL UNIT

Blue Steel high-level mission profile

Directional control of the missile was on the 'twist and steer' principle, in which each turn begins by rolling with the ailerons and is then maintained by increasing lift on the foreplanes. For the first part of the mission, the course was monitored continuously and the position determined by radar and astro-tracking equipment in the parent aircraft. At the moment the navigator flicked a switch, the computer inside the missile was told the exact position from which it was starting, its speed and the direction it was heading in. The missile fell freely and after a few seconds delay the rocket motor fired and the missile accelerated and began its climb. The inertial navigator in the missile then took over and computed every change of velocity and direction from ultra-sensitive acceleration measurements made within the missile, with reference to the position at which it left the carrier. Once launched, no signals from Blue Steel were required from outside and so it could not be jammed.

A further development of Blue Steel to meet a requirement to be launched at low level was met by a simple alteration to the missile and proved capable of being launched at 1000ft. The original missile was designed to cruise at 70,000–80,000ft. The low-level version of Blue Steel, known as W105A, would be released in a pop-up manoeuvre at 1,000ft and reach a height of more than 17,000ft. It had a range of 25–50 miles, as compared with the high-level version of up to 150 miles. At least one bomber in each squadron was maintained on constant ground combat duty.

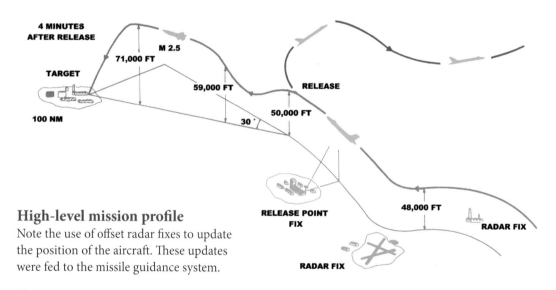

High-level mission profile
Note the use of offset radar fixes to update the position of the aircraft. These updates were fed to the missile guidance system.

The only Vulcan B.Mk1 (XA903) to carry the Blue Steel missile was used for test launches of the missile.

Blue Steel RAF service 1962–70

Service trials began in 1961 with the trials unit No. 4 JSTU based at Scampton being responsible for reporting all defects or unsatisfactory features on the missile and ground support equipment to Air Staff and the Ministry of Aviation (MoA). This was to allow the MoA to recommend clearance of the weapon system for release to service. The warhead capsule required little servicing by RAF personnel, the main servicing of this component being the responsibility of the AWRE. Several company representatives were based at Scampton during the trials and advised only to improve liaison between the service and industry.

The famous Dambusters of Lancaster bomber fame, No. 617 Squadron, was re-formed at Scampton in May 1958 to fly the Vulcan, joined by No. 83 Squadron in October 1960. In 1969, No. 230 OCU (operational conversion unit) arrived. Another Vulcan squadron was added to the station complement when No. 27 was re-formed in 1971, joined later by No. 35 Squadron.

The first B.Mk2 to be delivered to Scampton with a Blue-Steel-capable missile was XL317 in June 1962. It was given emergency operational capability in August 1962, two months before the Cuban Missile Crisis in October 1962. It was not until February 1963 that the missile was fully released for service. By the end of 1964, Nos. 83 and 27 Squadrons were equipped with Blue Steel, sharing weapons with Wittering's wing Nos. 139 and 100 Squadrons' Victor B2 aircraft. Blue Steel was officially retired on 31 December 1970 when the United Kingdom's strategic nuclear capacity passed to the Royal Navy's submarine fleet.

With the formation of Hawker Siddeley Dynamics Ltd in 1963, all missile work was to be centralised, and Blue Steel came under the Hawker Siddeley banner. The Avro Weapons Research Division left Woodford in 1965 to go to the nearby Stanley Green Business Park at Handforth Dean, Wilmslow, Cheshire, and remained there until 1971.

An operational Blue Steel missile showing its associated equipment at RAF Scampton.

Vulcan B.Mk2 XL321 of No. 617 Squadron with a Blue Steel missile pictured on 18 July 1962. The squadron's insignia was anti-flash roundel 'pink'.

Seen below in its low-level role is XL320 in its camouflage scheme on 16 December 1966.

More than 30 production B.Mk2 aircraft were modified to carry Blue Steel W100A and W103A missiles, along with three trials aircraft, B.Mk1 XA903, B.Mk2 XH538 and XH539. The production aircraft were fitted with both Olympus 201 and 301 series engines. These aircraft were XL317, XL318, XL319, XL320, XL321, XL359, Xl360, XL361, XL384, XL385, XL386, XL387, XL388, XL389, XL390, XL392, XL425, XL426, XL427, XL443, XL444, XL445, XL446, XM569, XM570, XM571, XM572, XM574, XM575, XM576, XM594 and XM595.

The Scampton wing eventually operated 33 Blue Steel aircraft. Modification kits were produced for fitment at RAF bases so that the aircraft could be converted to either a conventional or Blue Steel role.

Seen above in February 1963 is XL445 of 27 Squadron, which was based at RAF Scampton.

Further Blue Steel Missile Developments

The greatest criticism of the Blue Steel was its range, which led Avro to experiment further to improve the W100 missile. This involved a version with a smaller warhead, more compact guidance system and two rocket booster. This allowed more room for fuel and would have increased the range to 400 miles.

Further versions included the Mk1B, which used high-speed fuel; the Mk1C with external boosters; the Mk1D, a long-range Blue Steel powered by an improved Stentor rocket motor and two solid rocket boosters with external fuel tanks; the Mk1E using highly toxic hydrazine fuel; and the Mk1S with external-mounted fuel tanks.

An operating requirement (OR1149) was issued in May 1956 for a 1,000-mile missile with the last 100 miles flown at 100ft. Avro proposed the W112, which was to be powered by four ram jets designed to meet this requirement. This proved too ambitious for the time and a less demanding operating requirement (OR1159) was issued in May 1958. This was met by the W114, a modified version of Blue Steel W100, often referred to as Blue Steel Mk2. The new design carried two booster rockets on the upper surface of the body, designed to provide the propulsion of the missile after it was released from the aircraft at about M = 0.90. These provided the acceleration until the four Bristol Siddeley BRJ.824 ram jets on the wing tips became effective at M = 2.0. The boosters were then discarded. A nose plane effected longitudinal stability, and lateral stability was provided by means of a single fin placed on the lower surface of the model.

A 1/28-scale model was tested in the 3 x 3ft supersonic wind tunnel at the RAE in Thurleigh, Bedford, between August and September 1959. Tests were carried out with various combinations and at Mach numbers between M = 0.8 and 2.0. These experiments proved the integrity of the design.

The W114 had a planned increase in range of 1,000 miles or shorter and a speed of Mach 3.8–4. The internal guidance system was to be replaced by rear-mounted Doppler radar. This was a demanding specification and many difficulties were encountered with guiding the missile accurately over the required specified distance. After spending some £825,000, the project was cancelled in December 1959.

A mock-up of a further development of Blue Steel. It was a low-altitude-only version, with the rocket motor replaced by a 4,000lb thrust Viper turbojet fed by a ventral intake. It would have had a speed of Mach 0.9 and a range of 600nm at 500ft.

Blue Steel Mk2 (W114)

Often referred to as Blue Steel Mk2, the W114 was cancelled when it was decided to purchase the American Skybolt missile system in May 1960.

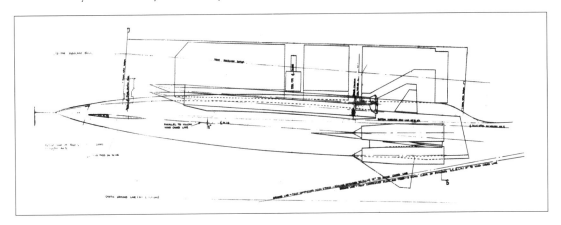

Above: An Initial Projects Department (IPD) drawing dated 5 December 1958 shows the installation of the W114 missile.

Right: W114 missile boost unit at the instant of jettison.

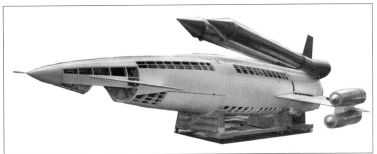

Skybolt Missile System

The United States Air Force (USAF) began accepting bids for the development of large ballistic missiles that could be launched from strategic bombers at high altitude in early 1959. Douglas Aircraft received the prime contract in May and in turn subcontracted to Northrop for the guidance system, Aerojet for the two-stage solid fuel propulsion system and General Electric for the re-entry vehicle. The system was initially known as WS-138A and was given the official name GAM-87 Skybolt in 1960. In May 1960, the British government agreed to purchase 144 Skybolt missiles. By agreement, British funding for research and development was limited to that required to modify the aircraft to take the missile, with Avro being selected as the UK main contractor. The first three B.Mk2 Vulcans allocated to be fitted out to carry the Skybolt missile were XH537, XH538 and XL391. The missile had a range of 1,150 miles with a flight ceiling of 300 miles and a speed of 9,500 miles per hour.

The Vulcans port and starboard wings were fitted with a hard point so that a pylon could be fitted to carry the missile. This pylon was strength tested at Whitworth Gloster Aircraft Company. In the bomb bay in the vicinity of the rear spar, a Douglas instrumented crate was used for the research and development.

The pylon and missile were similar to the Blue Jay/Gloster Javelin configuration. Extensive flight tests measuring the Blue Jay aerodynamic loads and comprehensive calculations on the flow field beneath the Javelin wing provided considerable groundwork for a reliable estimate of the aerodynamic loads on the Skybolt missile.

By 1961, several test missiles were ready for trialling from USAF B-52 bombers, with drop-tests starting in January. In England, compatibility trials with mock-ups started on the Vulcan. Powered tests started in the USA in April 1962, but the test series went badly, with the first five trials ending in a combination of dissimilar failures. The first successful launch of a Skybolt was on 19 December 1962.

Back at Avro, a report issued on 6 March 1962 stated that problems were encountered with flow visualisation testing around the Star Tracker window due to a large cross flow found to exist over the nose of the missile, which did not exist on the B-52 installation. This would have a serious effect on the missiles' navigation and involve extra personnel hours by Avro photographic personnel, which was not anticipated. This complication led to some 350 missile drops, compared with the anticipated 30.

By the time of the first fully successful flight in 1962, the American government had lost confidence in the project, leading to its cancellation. Avro received notice of the cancellation of contract KD/B/01/CB.6(a) for 40 Vulcan B.Mk2 Skybolt aircraft, along with contract KD/B/0118/CB.6(a) for Research and Development (R&D) work in early January 1963.

Aerodynamic trials were carried out by XH537 with two dummy Skybolts. On 9 December 1961, XH538 began dummy drop tests over the West Freugh range in Scotland.

Skybolt compatibility trials in the US

High above the Mojave Desert, near California, Avro Vulcan B.Mk2 (XH535) flies in formation with an American B-52 bomber. The Vulcan was piloted by Tony Blackman and 'Ossie' Hawkins. It was in America to take part in tests for the Skybolt installation. Like the Avro Vulcan, the B-52 was also to carry the Skybolt air-to-surface ballistic missile. It is interesting to note that, at time of writing, the B-52 is still in service with the USAF in its original high-level role.

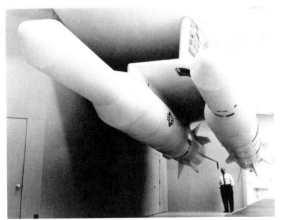 

Above left: Skybolt missiles under the Boeing B-52 wing mock-up, 14 April 1961.

Above right: A Boeing B-52 in formation with XH535. Note the difference in wing length.

Skybolt navigation system

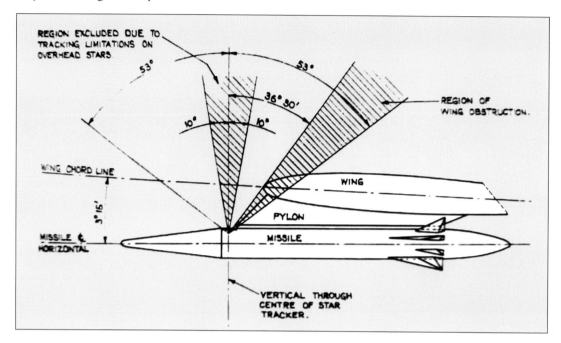

The Skybolt navigation system used an optical device known as Star Tracker, which measured the positions of stars. It was used to enhance the existing internal navigation system. Internal navigation systems at the time were not sufficiently accurate for intercontinental ranges. The missile would continually observe the sky. This requirement, along with ground clearance on take-off, presented a problem to other aircraft operated by the UK.

This led to the Vulcan being selected because it could mount the nose of the missile to project it in front of the Vulcan's delta wing. The Vulcan B.Mk2 was initially designed to carry two Skybolt ballistic missiles under the wing. The range of the missiles would be in the region of 1,150 miles. With the projected heavier UK Red Snow warhead, the range would be reduced to 600 miles with a speed of 9,500mph (Mach 12). The missile was 38ft 3in long, 3ft in diameter and weighed 11,000lb.

Shown below, XH537 is pictured on its first flight on 29 September 1961. Note the earlier shape of the Skybolt missile nose.

In November 1962, the Americans announced they were cancelling the Skybolt programme. A new replacement plan was hammered out that led to the Nassau Agreement on 21 December 1962 and to the United Kingdom purchasing the Polaris submarine-launched ballistic missile system equipped with British warheads.

The UK would thus retain its independent deterrent force, although its control passed from the RAF largely to the Royal Navy. The RAF kept its tactical nuclear capability.

A Skybolt dummy missile on XH537, pictured at Woodford, 21 September 1961.

Douglas Skybolt dummy missile installation. Note the later nose design.

Below: XH537 carrying Skybolt missiles, 17 October 1962. Note the new nose design carried on the port wing.

Type 698/5 Phase 6

The Air Staff was aware of the V-force's vulnerability to a first-strike attack. In 1960, Avro's Initial Projects Department produced a report (IPD 104) proposing the Vulcan be equipped to remain airborne for a longer duration so that, in an emergency, it could remain airborne in an area remote from risk of enemy attack. The total requirement included sufficient range to enable the Vulcan to proceed to and from the chosen targets and have an endurance of 13 to 14 hours. The specified armament was for four Douglas Skybolt missiles.

By having the deterrent force continually airborne, it would be virtually indestructible by the enemy, and comparison with other systems showed that the long-endurance aircraft provided the maximum deterrent for given expenditure.

The typical endurance of a Vulcan B.Mk2, with its current fuel capacity (the modification introducing long-range fuel tanks in the bomb bay not having been authorised) and with Olympus 200 engines, was seven hours with an internal weapon load. To raise this to the 13 to 14 hours required, with the addition of the weight and drag of the four missiles, was a formidable undertaking. The design proposals, designated Phase 6, comprised an increase in internal fuel capacity to more than double by fitting a large outer wing with partly integral and partly bag-fuel tankage, an increase in the lift-drag ratio by the greater span of a new outer wing, and the fitment of developed Olympus engines with improved specific fuel consumption. This was together with the possible fitment of aft fans, giving further improvement in specific fuel consumption and greater thrust at take-off. The increase in the weight of the missiles carried and the very substantial increase in fuel capacity increased the all-up weight of the proposed aircraft to about 350,000lb.

A Phase 6 report on 10 January 1962 consisted of a collection of current data. It replaced the previous data published in brochure IPD 104 and was in line with the information presented at the Air Ministry on 19 December 1961.

Phase 6 revised crew layout

The crew facilities outlined in IPD 104 were not considered suitable for an endurance of 13 to 14 hours. The addendum to IPD 104 included more space made available for the crew and ejection seats provided at all stations. This increased the basic operational weight by 3,840lb. As a result of the weight increase, the endurance was reduced by 12 minutes, without affecting take-off performance.

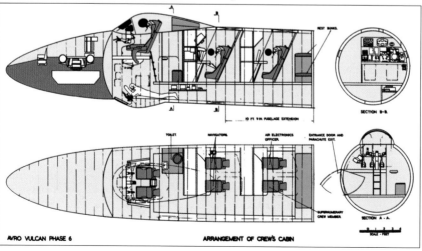

AVRO VULCAN PHASE 6 — ARRANGEMENT OF CREW'S CABIN

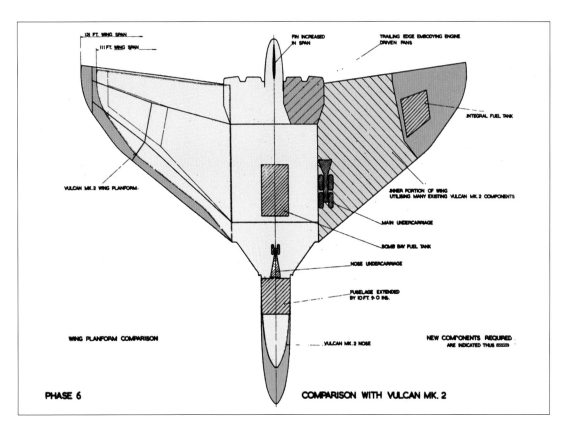

WING PLANFORM COMPARISON

PHASE 6

COMPARISON WITH VULCAN MK. 2

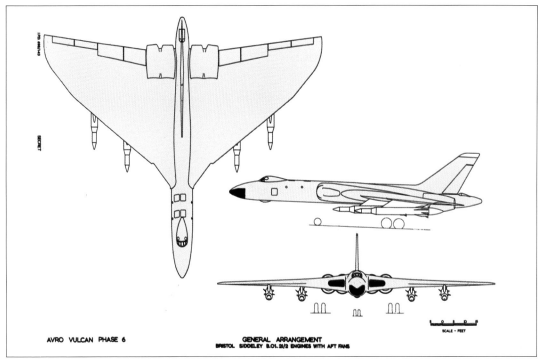

AVRO VULCAN PHASE 6

GENERAL ARRANGEMENT
BRISTOL SIDDELEY B.O1.21/2 ENGINES WITH AFT FANS

Rocket-Assisted Take-off Trials

To help overcome the performance problems of earlier jet engines in hot and high conditions, it was proposed to fit a rocket-assisted take-off gear (RATOG) system for the Valiant, Victor and Vulcan. This would allow the V-bomber force aircraft to maintain their operational weights from short runways and tropical conditions. The Vickers Valiant demonstrated RATOG at the Farnborough Airshow in 1957, powered by two de Havilland Super Sprite rocket engines. In May 1959 Vulcan B.Mk1 (XA889) was allotted to test this system. However, the RATOG system using the de Havilland Spectre was never tested on the Vulcan, although the Valiant and Victor did use it before the project was cancelled. The RATOG system never became operational for the V-force due to the increase in performance of the jet engine.

A study produced by the Avro Engineering Research Division and carried out by the Rocket Division of the de Havilland Engine Company in January 1961 reported to determine the effects of Spectre rocket-assisted take-off. A specimen rig was used, which consisted of a Vulcan Mk1 rear fuselage section from the rear spar aft and from rib 62.5 port to and including the inboard starboard elevator mounted on a steel dummy rear spar. Twenty-five tests were completed with a running time of approximately one minute. The report contained information on reflected vibration, noise and efflux on adjacent aircraft structure and operation efficiency of the DC and AC electrical system. The ATO system had been looked at for some time in various design reports from the 1950s to improve the take-off performance of aircraft. But with the change in operational requirement and improved performance of the Olympus engine, it was not required. On 14 July 1960, Victor XA930 successfully took off from Hatfield, assisted by two Spectre rocket pods between the port and starboard engines' intakes. This layout would have been a similar to that used by the Vulcan.

Shown below are pictures from the resultant engine tests completed by the de Havilland Engine Company on a specimen Vulcan rear fuselage and wing section.

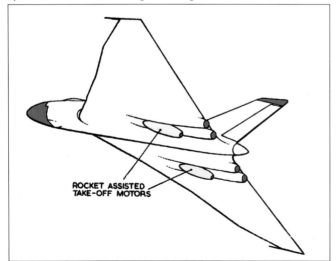

ROCKET ASSISTED
TAKE-OFF MOTORS

Quick Reaction Alert (QRA)

A design study was issued in January 1961 on alert readiness and rapid take-off requirements for the Vulcan pre-1963 B.Mk1/1A and B.Mk2 and post-1963 for the Vulcan B.Mk2 aircraft. Shown below are the requirements from that report.

Statement of policy and requirement

The Air Staff require that where the above aircraft are deployed on '30-day alert readiness', the rapid take-off capability shall be such as to meet the following warning timescale:

(a) Up to 1963, 15 minutes reducing to 3 minutes
(b) Post-1963, 30 seconds from inert to first aircraft rolling

These requirements are such as to dictate the need to achieve engine starting in the minimum possible time, and to ensure that connections to the aircraft from the various items of ground equipment necessary to ensure crew comfort, store conditioning, electrical supplies, etc., are kept to the absolute minimum and are capable of quick disconnection, with the minimum of ground crew attendance.

Adoption of QRA

Along with the adoption of QRA, the Vulcan would fly to dispersal bases around the United Kingdom to avoid being destroyed at its main bases.

QRA was inaugurated in February 1962, with Blue Steel squadrons forming the spearhead of Bomber Command's QRA force and was to do so for more than five years. The original procedure was to keep one aircraft from each squadron maintained in an armed condition. Staging points were constructed at the end of the runways, with aircraft parked on short strips to aid rapid take-off.

During a QRA, the ground crew would scramble from their nearby caravan, where they had been living, to their designated Vulcan. The crew chief would then check the pre-flighted aircraft, simultaneously starting all four engines by compressed air from the nearby Palouste. This was accomplished by pressing the rapid start button. The aircrew would then arrive and taxi the aircraft to the end of the runway and await instructions. It was not unknown for a QRA exercise to be trialled at 0300hrs on a Sunday. Four Vulcans could be scrambled within 90 seconds of starting to roll. During normal times, ground crews would live in their caravans for two weeks once a year as part of their QRA practice.

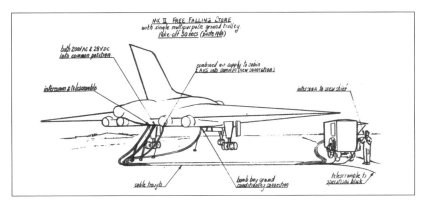

A Decade of Service

In June 1969 the first of the Blue Steel missiles were withdrawn, which led to the disbandment of the squadrons operating Blue Steel, starting with 83 Squadron on 19 July 1969. Towards the end of 1969 there were only five squadrons left in the United Kingdom operating the Vulcan: Nos. 27 and 617 at Scampton and Nos. 44, 50 and 101 Squadrons at Waddington continued in the tactical service of the Supreme Allied Commander Europe (SACEUR). The Cottesmore wing of Nos. 9 and 35 Squadrons moved to Akrotiri in Cyprus to provide back-up for NATO's Southern Flank and to provide support for Central Treaty Organisation (CENTO), originally known as the Middle East Treaty Organisation (or METO), if required. The last Vulcan Blue Steel sortie was with No. 617 Squadron on 21 December 1970.

Vulcan exercise at Scampton, 11 May 1961.
Inset: **Guard dogs were used to provide security on air bases operating the Vulcan.**

Change of Role

When Francis 'Gary' Powers, flying a Lockheed U2 as a covert surveillance aircraft, was brought down near Degtyarsk in the Ural region of the Soviet Union by SA-2 Guideline (S-75 Dvina) missiles on 1 May 1960, it became apparent that any high-flying aeroplane would be vulnerable to any surface-to-air missile defences. Intelligence reports indicated this would extend to the V-force and a requirement was issued to revert to the less vulnerable low-level role, which would delay detection by radar.

With the Valiant being phased out in 1964 due to metal fatigue and the Victor not being suitable for the low-level role, it was left to the Vulcan to fulfil this function, with its inherent stronger structure capable of withstanding the buffeting experienced at low level.

Low-level training began with B.Mk1A aircraft in April 1963, which became operational in June 1963. Vulcan B.Mk2 squadrons began training at the beginning of 1964 and were declared operational in May that year.

It was recognised that the resulting fatigue life would be affected by this role and a production B.Mk2 (XM596) was taken off the production line for structural testing, which led to strengthening modifications to allow the Vulcan to have a longer fatigue life of 12,000 hours in the low-level role. These structural modifications were completed at Bitteswell, Leicestershire, under a future remediable programme.

Camouflage

The first B.Mk2 Vulcan to have the new low-level camouflage scheme was XM645. It was to have a dark green and medium sea-grey upper surface and white anti-flash underside. The aircraft were usually given a glossy polyurethane finish. Particular attention was paid to providing the white underside a smooth finish; all rivets were made flush fitting and any gaps filled in. In the early 1970s, some aircraft were given a light aircraft-grey lower surface and the black radome began to disappear, in keeping with a general toning down.

When the Vulcan was manoeuvring at low level, it was found that the white anti-flash underside was clearly visible, so the Vulcan adopted an overall matt 'satin' camouflage scheme to make it less visible. Two aircraft in 1977 were a given a disruptive desert camouflage of sand and stone on the undersurface for the *Red Flag* exercise in the United States.

Pictured at low level, XM575 is flown on 10 August 1982 by Martin Withers, who flew the first mission by a Vulcan during the Falklands campaign.

Low-level Development

The RAF and Air Ministry looked at the idea of a low-level strategic bomber to avoid enemy radar in 1952, and the Ministry of Supply issued specification B126T to meet this requirement. The specification called for an aircraft that could deliver a 10,000lb nuclear bomb at an operational radius of 1,500 miles at a speed of Mach 0.85 and with at least 80 per cent of the mission flown at a height of 500ft. One of the earliest attempts to meet this specification was submitted by Avro in December 1952 and given the Type number 721. It was to have a range of 5,500 miles and a take-off weight of 124,000lb. Unlike the Vulcan, it had a very high-wing loading to satisfy its low-level role. The specification was later abandoned due to the technology not being available at the time to ensure accurate navigation, terrain following and low-level performance. In 1955, further studies were looked at, which led to the RAF's TSR2 and the Royal Navy's Blackburn Buccaneer.

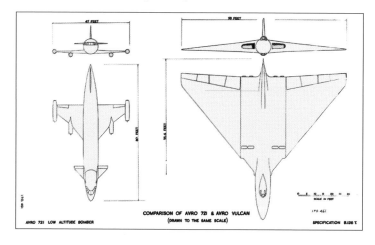

Tests were performed on the B.Mk2 set 60 (XM596) airframe to check that the structure fulfilled the requirements of SP.970 volume leaflet 200/4 and to establish the limit of serviceability of the aircraft under loads arising Flight Case 'C' of the flight envelope; 90.5 per cent of the test load was applied to the specimen without a major failure.

In 1964, the Air Staff issued requirement ASR380 for the Vulcan in the low-level role, reverting back to free-fall nuclear loads. Before terrain-following radar was introduced, Vulcan crews practised low-level flying using maps and the H2S radar. To help improve this capability to fly at low level, ARI5959 was introduced by Mod 2057, the General Dynamics terrain-following radar. Trials were carried out on Vulcan B.Mk2 XM606 from June 1965 and were cleared for service in 1966.

The system utilised an elevation monopulse 'on-bore sight' non-scanning technique to detect changes of terrain height immediately ahead of the aircraft's flight path. The system operated in conjunction with the FM Mk7B radio altimeter, the MFS equipment and various aircraft sensors and indicating and control units to produce pitch command signals, which assisted pilot manual control during low-level flight. The airborne radio installation (ARI) measured the slant range to terrain ahead of the aircraft, receiving inputs from other aircraft sensors and computing pitch control signals for display at the pilot's head-up indication pitch plane, to give a resultant flight path that followed the rise and fall of the terrain at the pre-selected altitude adjustable between 200 and 1,000ft. The installation provided safe low-level terrain following over land, water and manmade obstacles within specified limits.

The radar section of the installation measured 'range to terrain' (R) along the fixed depression angle of the radar beam, while the FM Mk7B radio altimeter accurately measured height above terrain (H). This information, range (R) and height (H), was compared in the terrain-following radar (TFR) computer with a reference range (r) and a reference height (h). The (r) was pre-programmed into the computer to suit the flying characteristics of the aircraft and the (h) was selected at a height selector switch on the TFR control unit.

When the measured values of (H) or (R) deviated from the references (h) and (r), as a result of changes in terrain, a corresponding pitch-up or pitch-down signal was generated and displayed at the pilot's head-up display (HEAD-UP indicator) or head-down display (MFS director horizon). The pilot was thus able to alter the altitude of the aircraft in the pitch plane to null the climb or dive indication and thereby cause the aircraft to follow the rise and fall of the terrain. This technique is illustrated below.

TFR mode of operation

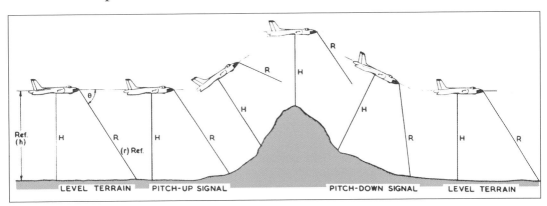

The TFR comprised an 8in-diameter, 36in-long pod immediately below the flight-refuelling probe. Post-Mod 2395, the length of the pod was increased by 7.6in to accommodate a filter unit. The forward end of the pod, which projects into the airstream, housed a microwave aerial sub-assembly, while the rear end of the probe enclosed by the aircraft nose contained the associated transmitter-receiver, signal processing, computing and power pack sub-assemblies.

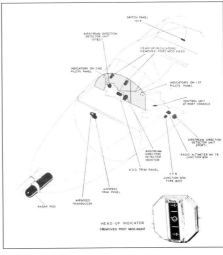

The Concorde Connection

Not only was the Vulcan powered by the Olympus, which was developed for use on Concorde and tested on XA903 (shown below), it was also used along with the Type 707 aircraft in the development of materials, aerodynamics and flying systems for the Concorde programme.

Because of the large delta wing, low-flying characteristics and being more representative of the inertia weight of Concorde, Vulcan B.Mk1 XA890, still with its straight wing, was operated by the Aerodynamics Research Flight at RAE Bedford to prove the use of the Concorde 'Ogee' slender wing planform to overcome the problems of low-speed handling on take-off with engine failure. The specialists developed the take-off director (TOD) system, which was extensively tested on XA890 to help overcome these problems; it was also used to show commercial pilots how the system worked.

The aircraft had arrived at RAE Bedford in January 1964 after completing radio, radar and armament trials and flew some 100 hours evaluating the TOD system. The aircraft was taken off charge on 12 September 1969.

Engine development

Avro Vulcan B.Mk1 XA903 first flew on 10 May 1957 and was used for Blue Steel development trials. In late 1962 it was re-allotted for APU development. On 3 January 1964 it went to Bristol Siddeley Engines Ltd at Filton for conversion to an Olympus 593 flying test bed. This engine was a further development of the Olympus 22R and was being worked up for the Concorde programme. It made its first flight on 9 September 1966 and by 1971 had completed more than 400 hours flying hours with the 593 engine.

On 4 August 1971, XA903 arrived at Marshalls of Cambridge for conversion of the pod to allow fitment of the Rolls-Royce RB.199 engine. This engine was being developed for the multi-role Tornado, which would eventually provide the RAF with the bombing and reconnaissance roles provided by the Vulcan. It was delivered to Rolls-Royce in February 1972 and made its first flight with the RB.199 on 19 April 1973. In 1976, it was used for ground-firing trials of a Mauser 27mm cannon made from the RB.199 pod before it completed its trials in 1971. On 22 February 1979, it arrived at the RAE at Farnborough for ground training before it was struck off charge on 19 July 1979. The nose was acquired by Wellesbourne Wartime Museum at Wellesbourne Mountford Airfield near Stratford-upon-Avon.

Outside Support

In this section, it is worth mentioning the work of the Repair and Servicing Department CWP (Contractors and Servicing Working Party) based at Bracebridge Heath, Lincolnshire. The department's function was first formed in 1941 to support Avro-built aircraft in the field. The department's personnel were permanently out working in the UK and overseas.

In 1943, Bracebridge Heath had its own design office, manned by a small team led by Gilbert Whitehead, who became Divisional Technical Director for the Manchester Division before retiring in 1979, in order to support the main design office at Woodford on repair drawings and modification work of Manchester-built aircraft in service with the RAF. The department was later expanded and included the support of civilian aircraft.

In April 1982, it was announced that Bracebridge Heath was to close as a result of reductions in MoD expenditure.

This Vulcan from RAF Finningley made a wheels-up 'pancake' landing during a midnight training flight in 1965. After removal from the runway, the CWP workers repaired the aircraft to fly with the squadron again.

RAF St Athan

On 6 September 1978, a major milestone was reached when personnel at St Athan celebrated the completion of the 500th major servicing of a 'V' aircraft – Vulcan XM573. The occasion represented a double milestone as the handing over of the Vulcan to the crew from No. 230 OCU for delivery to RAF Waddington coincided with the 40th anniversary of the inauguration of St Athan as an RAF base.

Last Vulcan Major Service

On 21 May 1981, RAF St Athan bid farewell to the last Vulcan bomber, XL426, to have a major service. Major servicing on the Vulcan began at St Athan in 1962 – then it was the B.Mk1. A total of 31 Mk1 types were majored during the next four years before the B.Mk2 appeared at the base in 1966. XL426 was the 267th B.Mk2 to have a major service.

For those who like statistics, 27,500 man-hours were expended on one major service. So the total 'cost' at St Athan was approximately eight million man-hours over a 19-year period. Turnaround time started at 46 days but increased to 56 as the aircraft grew older. One major service involved 85 highly skilled personnel. Major servicing was carried out every 1,280 flying hours.

During the ceremony, XL426 was handed back to Gp Capt V L Warrington, Officer Commanding RAF Scampton, where the aircraft was based, by the Air Officer Commanding Maintenance Units Headquarters, Support Command, Air Vice-Marshal D W Richardson and Air Commodore Geof Tyler, Station Commander at St Athan.

XL426 later went to No. 50 Squadron at RAF Waddington in 1982 and later became part of the Station Flight in 1984 for the Vulcan Display Flight. In 1986, it was sold to Mr R Jacobson and delivered to Southend Airport on 19 December 1986.

Systems Summary

Hydraulic system

The hydraulic system was electrically controlled and operated the alighting gear, bomb doors, wheel brakes and nose-wheel steering. A reserve pressure supply for the brakes was retained by two accumulators charged from the main hydraulic system. An electro-hydraulic power pack was available for the emergency operation of the bomb doors and to recharge the brake system when the hydraulic pumps were not operating. When certain special stores were carried, an independent electrically driven hydraulic power pack was fitted in the bomb bay.

Compressed air system

A compressed air system was installed to lower the alighting gear in an emergency. A further compressed air system was provided to open or close the main entrance door and also to initiate jettisoning of the canopy.

Air-conditioning equipment

The air-conditioning system was installed to maintain the air in the crew's compartment at reasonable temperatures and pressures. Air from the engine compressors was used for pressurisation and heating, the flow of air being automatically maintained by flow controllers. Air-conditioning equipment in the nose wheel bay controlled the temperature of the air entering the cabin and the pressure in the cabin was maintained by pressure controllers that regulated the amount of air allowed to pass into the atmosphere through discharge valves. Provision was also made for cabin ventilation during unpressurised flight. A further air-conditioning system, supplied with engine compressor air, was fitted in the bomb bay when certain special stores were carried.

De-icing system

Thermal de-icing provides protection against ice accretion on the wing, fin and engine air intake leading edges; hot air for the systems was bled off the engine compressors and mixed with cold air to give a controlled temperature for distribution. A further system, utilising de-icing fluid, was provided for the pilots' and air bomber's windscreens.

Fuel

Fuel was carried in 14 bag-type tanks contained in magnesium-alloy compartments, four tanks in the fuselage and five in each outer wing. Each tank was equipped with contents gauge transmitters, electrically operated fuel pumps, a maximum fuel-level cut-off switch and refuelling valves. In addition, No. 1 and No. 7 tanks each had a transfer pump, which could be used to balance the fuel load should the aircraft become nose or tail heavy. The tanks were arranged in groups so that each engine was normally fed by a particular group of tanks. Cross-feed cocks were provided so that in an emergency any engine could receive fuel from any tank or group of tanks. All tanks were pressurised to prevent vaporisation and consequent loss of fuel at altitude, with air from the engine compressors being used for this purpose. To protect the tanks from internal fires or explosions, a Graviner explosion-protection system was fitted. A pressure-refuelling system was provided, in which the distribution of fuel load among all the tanks was automatically controlled to ensure correct aircraft loading.

Fire protection

The fire protection system consisted of two separate methyl-bromide installations, one for the engines and the other for the fuel tank bays. Hand-operated water glycol extinguishers were placed at convenient positions in the crew's compartment.

Airborne equipment

Additional airborne equipment was mounted in the rear fuselage. Temperature control of the ECM canisters was affected by water/glycol and vapour cycle heat control systems, while the tail warning unit, which formed the fuselage rear cone, was provided with pneumatic and cooling systems. Three doors on the underside of the rear fuselage gave access to this equipment. Counterpoise plates of honeycomb construction were mounted below the starboard centre engine rib, between the jet pipe curvatures.

Electrical power was supplied by four 40kVA 200-volt 3-phase 400 c/s AC engine-driven alternators, arranged to supply independent load or in parallel via a synchronising ring main system. Reserve power was supplied from the auxiliary airborne power plant or the RAT at 200-volt 3-phase 400 c/s AC power and 115-volt 3-phase 400 c/s AC was provided, through various transformers, from the 200-volt system and from the same source by means of two frequency changers. A supply at 115-volt single-phase 1600 c/s AC was also available. DC power was provided at 28 volts through two 7.5kVA transformer rectifier units and a single 24-volt battery provided sufficient power for crash and emergency services. A ground supply plug was provided on the port side aft fuselage for the 200-volt AC system and two 28-volt plugs were provided, adjacent to the nose-wheel bay for ground-servicing supply. In the unlikely event of the failure of all four alternators, sufficient power to maintain control would be available from the APUs.

Special instrument

To enable the crew to scan areas to the rear, above and below the aircraft, a Kelvin Hughes rear-viewing periscope was installed at the navigator's station.

Wireless

Wireless equipment consisted of general-purpose HF (under control of the AEO), UHF, ILS and twin VHF installations (controlled by the navigator). A low-range radio altimeter provided indication for, and was controlled by, the first pilot. A high-range radar altimeter provided indication for, and was controlled by, the navigator/air bomber. Radar installations consisting of Gee, Green Satin, tail warning, IFF, navigation bombing system (NBS) and ECM were fitted. Intercommunication between crew members was provided by a separate system, with switching facilities for introducing radio signals and conference intercom. Five aerials were fitted externally to the fuselage, consisting of two UHF, two IFF and one VHF. The HF transmitter-receiver was fed with signals from a resonant slot in the aircraft fin. The ILS installation had three aerials, two being tuned notches (one in each wing tip) and the third, a tuned metal strip contained in a box fitted below the No. 2 starboard tank bay. The automatic direction finder (ADF) utilised a loop aerial contained in a shallow dish, which was fitted in the bomb bay roof, and the radio and radar altimeter installations used recessed reflector-type aerials. The H2S installation employed a rotating scanner in the nose.

Crew accommodation

The Vulcan was equipped to carry five crew members, although a sixth seat was provided with an oxygen probe/to lead and static line. A ventilated suit system was provided for the five crew members, the air for which was tapped from the main cabin pressurisation system.

Modification 1696 introduced swivel seats for the rear crew members. The navigator/radar and the AEO were provided with swivel seats and the navigator/plotter had a modified static seat. Each seat embodied an assisted cushion and carried a Mk46 parachute, incorporating demand emergency oxygen set. All three seats could slide fore and aft on rails.

Guidance systems

Navigation and bombing system – 1971

The Vulcan was fitted with the Mk1A navigation bombing system (NBS 1A), autopilot Mk10, MFS, true airspeed unit (TASU) and heading reference system (HRS) Mk2. The equipment did not contain any inertial sensing devices.

The ARI utilised the Doppler techniques to compute along and across heading velocity data, determining ground speed, drift angle and distance gone for display. This data was also routed to the aircraft's HRS. The Green Satin Doppler radar navigation aid had been used since the early days of the Vulcan and was later updated to the more reliable Green Satin Mk2.

By 1970, Green Satin had been replaced by ARI 5972, introduced by Mod 2256. This comprised a 'J'-band lightweight navigational radar aid, which could operate under all flight conditions to determine accurate navigational data. The ARI was

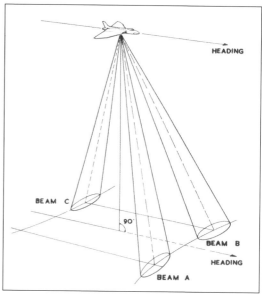

Airborne Doppler system – ARI 5972. Heading information was displayed at the navigator's/plotter's position.

a compact installation comprising a transmitter-receiver and aerial unit and a control indicator. The installation operated between altitudes of 15,000ft and 60,000ft in all weather conditions and in limited pitch-and-roll configurations over land or sea. Use of the Doppler technique eliminated inaccuracies resulting from rough terrain. A built-in facility permitted manual correction of errors arising from increased refraction and scatter encountered over calm water.

The navigation and bombing system Mk1A was used in medium- and long-range aircraft beyond the range of ground aids. The system was primarily used for accurate radar blind bombing but incorporated facilities for rapid fixing, wind finding and homing, thus relieving the navigator of many of the calculations involved in dead reckoning (DR) navigation. The complete system comprised two distinct sub-systems:

    (a) H2S Mk9A (primary radar) was developed and produced by Electrical & Musical Instruments (EMI).

    (b) Navigation and bombing computer (NBC) Mk2 was produced by Associated Electrical Industries Ltd.

H2S scanner

The antenna was used for both transmission and reception of signals; it rotated through 360° at a rate that varied with each scale. The rate was 32rpm on 1/8 and 1/4 million, 16rpm on 1/2 million and 8rpm on 1 million. The scanner could be made to sweep a selected sector instead of rotating through 360°, the size and bearing of the sector being set by the operator.

The scanner could also be tilted downwards to give a clearer picture at shorter ranges. The scanner assembly was stabilised in pitch and roll by an earth-tied, giro-controlled servo system, so that within certain limits, the display was not affected by aircraft attitude.

A secondary radar system provided automatic identification as a 'friendly' when the aircraft was properly challenged by a suitably equipped ground or airborne radar. A coded reply, independent of the mode of interrogation, was provided as an emergency signal and indicated that the aircraft was in distress.

A further system, ARI 5924, was introduced that radiated interrogation pulses and received a reply and identification pulses from the ARI 5922 fitted in tanker aircraft. The information was displayed continuously on a cathode ray tube screen of an indicator unit. The trace provided range, heading and identification information at distances up to a maximum of 100 nautical miles and a minimum of 400 yards.

Airborne Doppler system ARI 5972 heading information was displayed at the navigator's/plotter's position.

Dead reckoning (DR) navigation computing

The NBC could be split into the following systems: (a) DR navigation computing, (b) steering and range computing, (c) ballistic computing, (d) height computing.

The navigation computer had the following inputs: (a) heading from the MFS, (b) true airspeed from the TASU, (c) wind velocity from wind monitor unit or handset. From this information, it calculated the track, ground speed and integrated ground movement, north–south and east–west. Track, ground speed and true airspeed were displayed at the navigator's panel.

TACAN

The TACAN replaced the Gee Mk3 radio navigation aid and was a worldwide navigation aid that provided the following information: magnetic bearing of the aircraft from a selected beacon, slant range of the aircraft from a selected beacon in nautical miles, and a flag alarm circuit that operated in the absence of correct distance signals. It was also used in the air-to-air role to provide range information between aircraft.

Astro navigation

Astro navigation was an integral part of the navigation techniques. It was used to monitor the ground position indicator (GPI) when other aids were not available, i.e., over large sea areas. It was also used as a standby in the event of failure of the NBS and MFS systems. Problems associated with this system were accurate readings in turbulent conditions and daylight readings with only the sun being available.

Autopilot and landing system

The Mk10A/Mk10B autopilot was provided in the aircraft to relieve the pilot of much of the physical and mental strain to which he was subjected when controlling high-speed bombing during long flights. The autopilot also improved the stability of the aircraft under difficult flying conditions.

The system operated on the 'rate-rate' principle and would stabilise an aircraft on each of the pitch, roll and yaw axes. In addition, the autopilot could be used by the pilot to change an aircraft's heading or attitude, maintain a constant altitude or indicated airspeed, turn on to and maintain a pre-selected heading or make fully automatic approaches to an airfield equipped with an ILS.

During bombing runs, the autopilot could also be used to manoeuvre the aircraft in response to signals from the NBS Mk1A or from a turn controller by the air bomber. Bombing, heading and radio information were passed to the system via the MFS, with which the autopilot was integrated.

With the deletion of the automatic landing facility on the Mk10B autopilot, the Mk10B functioned in the same way as the Mk10A autopilot.

INSTINCTIVE CUT-OUT SWITCH
ON PILOTS COLUMN

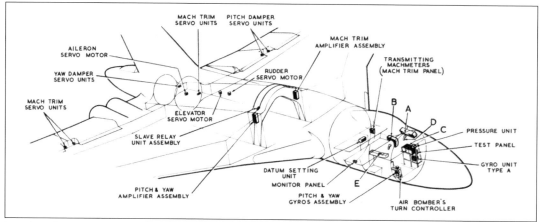

Location of auto-controls.

Ballistic computing

Ballistic information relevant to the type of bomb carried was contained in a short piece of 35mm film. Information from the film was fed into the calculator Type 3 Mk1, which was connected to the static line of the starboard pitot-static system. The equipment then operated to calculate the required track to the release point steering signals, which were fed to the MFS via the bombing system selector switch and the MFS selector switch. These signals were then displayed on the azimuth directors and could be interlocked with the Mk10A or 10B autopilot through the computer unit (navigational) of the MFS signals to open the bomb doors and release the bomb.

Mounted immediately above the indicating unit type 301 was a camera that photographed the plan position indicator (PPI) at intervals of eight seconds throughout the bombing run. The film was marked automatically at the moment of bomb release and would continue to photograph the PPI until completion of the bombing run.

The aircraft could be guided along a pre-determined track for a bombing run, by signals from either the bomb aimer's controller or the NBC, operating through the autopilot.

Opening the bomb doors caused extra drag on the aircraft fuselage resulting in a nose-down pitch error. Provision was made in the autopilot and aircraft wiring for compensating signals to be applied to the elevator servo channel and also disconnection of the pitch monitor, which resulted in elevator movement. This movement corrected the aircraft trim so that steady flight was maintained. Compensation was not applied once the doors were fully open or while they were closing.

Pitot-static system

The pitot-static installation embraced two independent systems, one port and one starboard. The starboard system connected to the NBS calculator Type 3, the MFS manometric unit and the bombsight computer.

At the front spar, the starboard system connected to the bomb fuse switch and ground test valve. The fatigue meter airspeed switch and VG recorder were fed by the starboard system. The port system fed the artificial feel warning switches, and the starboard system fed the three artificial feel units. These units were linked to the flying control rods and their action was controlled by actuators operating in conjunction with transmitter units that were sensitive to airspeed. The pilots' instruments on the first pilot's panel were supplied by the starboard system; this included the pressure – ASI and Mach meter, static – ASI Mach meter, altimeter and rate of climb indicator. A duplicate set of instruments on the second pilot's panel was supplied by the starboard system.

Three airspeed indicators were fitted in the aircraft along with three altimeters, one on each pilot's panel and one each on the plotter's panel at the navigator's station.

Pitot head mounting.

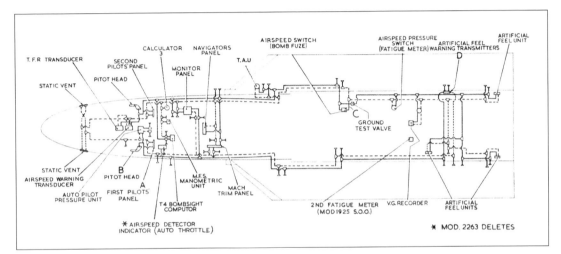

Pitot-static system.

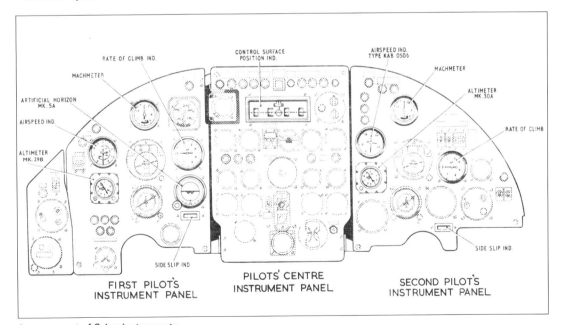

Arrangement of flying instruments.

Dorsal aerial

A multi-channel transmitter-receiver provided radio telephone, carrier wave or data communication within the high-frequency band from 2MHz to 30MHz. The equipment could transmit or receive on any one of 28,000 selected carrier frequencies spaced at intervals of 1KHz. The unit was controlled by unit Type M53 located at the port side of the navigator's panel. The aerial was of the suppressed type fitted to the lower part of the dorsal fin.

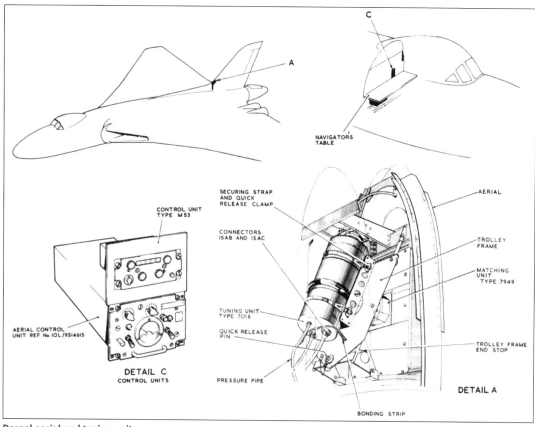

Dorsal aerial and tuning unit.

Airborne UHF installation

The ARI 18124/2 was an airborne UHF installation designated R/T2, consisting of a multi-channel transmitter and receiver operating on a crystal-controlled frequency range of 225.0MHz to 399.9MHz with facilities available to radiate MCW for emergency or direction-finding purposes. The ARI also incorporated a simulated bombing tone for tactical training on Vulcan aircraft. Two UHF aerials were located, one below the bomb aimer's window and the upper aerial above No. 1 bomb bay and fitted externally on the aircraft. A control unit was fitted on the port console.

Airborne automatic direction

Airborne direction-finding equipment provided automatic relative-bearing indication from source radio signals. Aerial relative-bearing determination was by null signal method, the loop aerial being remotely controlled and aerial reception of modulated or un-modulated radio signals, either by loop or sense aerial.

The unit was controlled at the navigator's station. Other controls consisted of a loop controller and a bearing and tuning indicator. In addition, a second bearing and tuning indicator was provided on the second pilot's panel. A change-over switch was provided. ADF/TACAN/ILS was located on the port console.

The sense aerial was an omni-directional type and was used initially for the reception of a broadcast station prior to actual direction finding by the loop aerial and associated ADF equipment. This aerial was also used for ARI-23180 on aircraft in the maritime reconnaissance (MR) role.

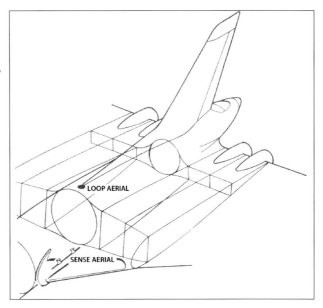

Long-range navigation (LORAN)

The LORAN ARI-23180 installation was fitted to aircraft in the MR role. The equipment provided a navigation fix with respect to a chain of ground-transmitting stations. The LORAN system used a pulse technique hyperbolic position fixing aid. LORAN group-transmitting stations included a master station and two, three or four slave stations. Transmissions propagated from the master station were received at each slave station and any receiver within the service area. Each slave station delayed by a precise time interval known as the coding delay and then transmitted its own signal.

Instrument landing system (ILS)

ARI-18011 was an airborne ILS operating in conjunction with ground transmitters. This installation provided the pilot with indications of the aircraft's position relative to the runway touch-down point, when descending to low altitude in bad visibility. The signals were received by the localiser and glidepath receiver units and fed via a junction box to the navigator's computer unit. Signals so received were displayed on the beam compass and director horizon instruments, which were also used in conjunction with the MFS.

Radar altimeter

The radar altimeter ARI-18090 employed a pulse radar technique to measure the height of the aircraft above the terrain immediately beneath the aircraft, through a range of 500 to 50,000ft.

Intercommunications system (i/c)

The comprehensive intercommunication system (ARI-18089) was a service-selecting system that provided three distinct but correlated functions: (1) to provide a channel for distribution of normal and conference i/c, (2) to provide a means of selecting all available ARIs, (3) to provide a means of mixing two or more receiver services, without one adversely affecting the other.

In addition, external i/c facilities were available as an aid to the ground crew during servicing and as a means of alerting the crew for tele-scramble operations. The installation was divided into two systems: normal i/c and conference i/c, each having its own amplifier.

Camera installation

An F95 Mk4 camera was fitted under Mod 2502 to maritime radar reconnaissance role (MRR) aircraft.

The camera was mounted over the window at the prone bomb aimer's position. A control unit, operated by the navigator/bomber remotely controlled the camera functions. It replaced the F95 Mk9 camera used for low-level bomb scoring.

Rear warning radar

By 1972 the Vulcan incorporated the Red Steer Mk2 ARI 5952 X-Band search radar

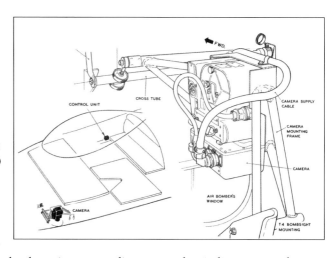

system. The ARI consisted of a tail-mounted radar unit, scanner alignment and an indicator azimuth range unit mounted at the navigator's station. The latter unit combined the functions of an indicator and control unit. When airborne, the ARI would normally be maintained in a standby condition (not transmitting) for most of the time. This was due to the operation of other ECM equipment. When required, the ARI could be switched to transmit in order to find the exact range and bearing of the attacking aircraft.

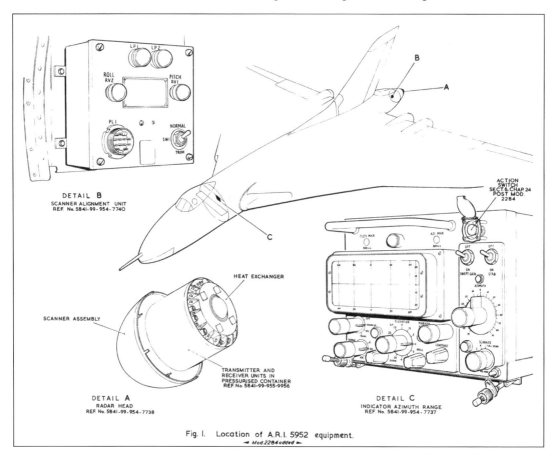

Fig. I.   Location of A.R.I. 5952 equipment.

T4 bombsight and armament instruments

The T4 bombsight was mounted centrally on the aircraft floor at the air bomber's prone position. It was a visual impact bombsight that was designed to commute and indicate continuously (at the instant of bomb release) the point on the ground that would be struck by the bomb. The sight was designed to utilise the accurate ground speed and drift angle supplied by the aircraft's Doppler equipment. When ARI 5972 was fitted in lieu of ARI 5951 (Mod 2256), there was no supply of ground speed and drift angle information to the bombsight.

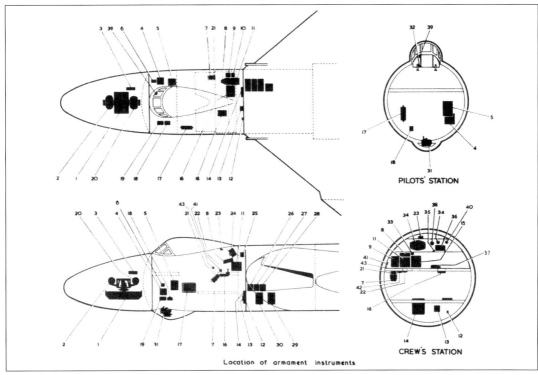

Location of armament instruments

1. SCANNER UNIT TYPE 121	23.	VARIABLE AIRSPEED UNIT, MK3
2. AMPLIFIER A3703	24.	NAVIGATIONAL PANEL, MK1B
3. AMPLIDYNE A3XX1	25.	WIND UNIT, MK2
4. CALCULATOR, TYPE 2, MK2	26.	POWER UNIT, TYPE 729
5. CALCULATOR, TYPE 3, MK1	27.	CALCULATOR ATUOMATIC 5A
6. GROUND SPEED RESOLVER	28.	WAVEFORM GENERATOR, TYPE 68B
7. CONTROL UNIT, TYPE 12580A	29.	CALCULATOR, TYPE 1, MK1
8. CAMERA, TYPE R110 OR R88	30.	POWER UNIT, MK2
9. CONTROL UNIT, TYPE 595	31.	T4 BOMBSIGHT SIGHTING HEAD (inoperative Post-Mod 2256 and 2377)
10. CONTROL UNIT (CAMERA), TYPE 903		
11. INDICATING UNIT, TYPE 301D	32.	BOMBING INDICATOR, MK1
12. SUPPRESSOR, TYPE G5	33.	WIND INDICATOR
13. RESISTANCE UNIT MK1	34.	FORWARD THROW INDICATOR
14. JUNCTION BOX, TYPE 343	35.	STEERING SIGNAL TEST JB
15. CONTROL UNIT, TYPE 585C	36.	TRACK CONTROL UNIT
16. CONTROL UNIT, TYPE 12558	37.	GPI, MK6
17. *T4 BOMBSIGHT COMPUTER	38.	COMPASS REPEATER, TYPE B
18. *T4 BOMBSIGHT SIGHTING HEAD CONTROL PANEL	39.	SFOM GUNSIGHT TYPE 812 A
19. *T4 BOMBSIGHT GYRO CONTROL J	40.	PILOTS' DIRECTIONAL INDICATOR
20. MODULATOR, TYPE 2	41.	CONTROL UNIT, TYPE 6204
21. BOMBING SELECTOR SWITCH	42.	JUNCTION BOX, TYPE 6205
22. CONTROL UNIT, TYPE 626	43.	VOLTMETER

*Inoperative Post-Mod 2256 and 2377.

Warning and Counter Measures – 1974

Rainbow codes were a series of code names used until 1958. They were replaced by alphanumeric numbers: ARI stands for 'airborne radio installation', followed by alphanumeric numbers.

The ECM equipment fitted to B.Mk1A and B.Mk2 Vulcans was designed to operate against EW/GCI radars, VHF communications and AI radar. The installation consisted of three jammers, a tail warning radar, a radar-warning receiver and two window dispensers. The majority of the equipment was housed in the rear section of the fuselage and all control was exercised from the AEO's station.

Blue Diver (ARI 18075) was used to jam metric ground radars. The installation was designed to transmit randomly keyed pulses of RF noise. The noise transmission, derived from a white noise source, was switched on and off automatically at irregular intervals of a few seconds' duration. Two transmitters were fitted.

Green Palm (ARI 18074) was a VHF jammer. One transmitter was carried, which radiated continuously on one frequency or in sequence at random intervals on two or four frequencies. The radiation was on spot frequencies, designed to jam individual channels and was tuneable in the air.

Red Shrimp (ARI 18076) was a high-band jamming system. It had three aerials mounted on two counterpoise plates on the structure between No. 3 and No. 4 engine jet pipes on the lower surface and operated in the centimetric and S-band frequencies. There were up to three transmitters and power units in canisters in the rear fuselage. A control unit at the AEO station controlled the three transmitters and power units.

Blue Saga (ARI 18105) allowed the AEO to monitor aurally any radar pulses illuminating the aeroplane; it also gave a visible and audible warning when persistently illuminated by a lock-follow radar. To prevent radar equipment in the aeroplane giving spurious indications on Blue Saga, blanking units were used that muted the receiver for each pulse of H2S, Red Steer and Green Satin. Each pair of aerials (one 'S'-band and one 'X'-band) fed the one receiver located nearby. The receiver outputs were fed to a control indicator.

Red Steer (ARI 5919) was an X-band tail warning radar and gave a 90° cone, up to a range of 15–18 miles. The display was unstabilised and gave a range and bearing relative to the bomber centreline. It replaced Orange Putter in 1957.

The aerials for the metric jammers were in notches in the wing tips. The VHF jammer used the helmet-type aerial in the top of the tail fin. In the aircraft where this was also used for VHF communications, a change-over relay was fitted.

Window: the window-dispensing equipment consisted of a control unit at the AEO's station and two stripper units. Only one stripper unit could be used at the same time and could dispense continuously at a pre-set rate, or in bursts of a pre-set duration and intervals. Window would be used for general confusion of ground radars, or to break a lock-follow radar.

ECM trials aircraft

During 1972 Vulcan B.Mk2 (XM597) was used as a trials aircraft for ARI 18228. This entailed the removal from the aircraft of the Blue Saga installation (ARI 18105) and the installation of RF head and antenna stacks at each end of the fin cap. This equipment was supplied by Marconi Space and Defence Systems Ltd at Stanmore, Middlesex.

Compatibility trials were completed at Woodford with XM597 during August 1972, with a service feed in by the end of 1973.

The following is a list of airborne radio installations fitted to XM597 in 1972:

IFF/SSR (1600 series), ARI-(23134), Red Steer Mk2 (5952), Doppler Decca 72 (5972), TACAN (18107/13) TFR (5959), ILS (18011), HF/SSB Collins 618T-3 (23090), Intercom and Audio Warning (18089), UHF ARC 52 (18124/2), ADF (23023), Mk7B Rad, Alt. Low Level (23172) Rad, Alt. High Level (18090), PTR 175 VHF/UHF (23143), NBC Mk1A comprising H2S Mk9B and NCB Mk2A (5928), Blue Diver (Metric Jammer) (18075), 'X'-Band Jammer (18146), Airborne Warning System (18228/1), 'L'-Band Jammer (18205}.

The ARI provided visual and audio warning of illumination by radar operating in the tracking mode. It identified the radar signal and provided directional and frequency band information of the illumination.

The trials aircraft was also used in Operation *Corporate* during the Falklands crisis in 1982, where it also used the American anti-radar Shrike missile.

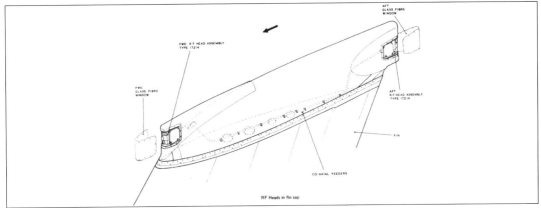

ARI 18228/1 radar-warning receiver, which replaced the Blue Saga jamming installation.

Red Light (ARI 18146), shown below, was a barrage jammer operating on the X-band frequencies. It scanned the X-band for threats and locked on to the signal to be jammed. The aerials were enclosed by a small radome at the rear fuselage.

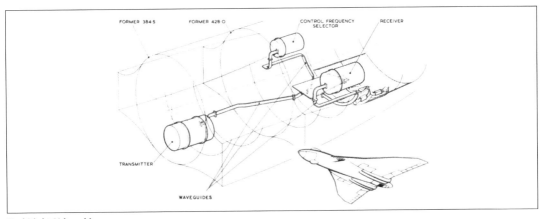

Red Light X-band jammer.

Strategic Reconnaissance (SR) Role

On 23 February 1971, Avro formally applied to the Ministry of Aviation Supply for contract cover for a feasibility study for the Vulcan B.Mk2 in the strategic reconnaissance (SR) role. The study proposed that the Avro Vulcan should replace Victors in the SR role to contract K6A/128/V. This required an improved H2S NBC radar with data handling, a LORAN aid, an air-monitoring facility and improved photographic facilities. An earlier contract for an air-monitoring system dated 5 March 1970 stated that the pod would use Skybolt pick-ups for the pod forward suspension. The eight aircraft originally nominated for the SR role embraced this particular Skybolt modification. Long-range navigation was satisfied by the incorporation of the LORAN 'C' ADL 21 equipment, comprising an aerial, amplifier, CRT indicator and read-out unit. Kelvin Hughes was to be responsible for the data handling and proposed radar display, which used the existing naval radar, Type 1006. It was presumed that the bombing facility would not be required and the NBS would be retained other than for the double offset bombing unit, the armament panel 9p and the time-delay unit of the low-level visual-release system.

Nine B.Mk2 aircraft were converted to the MR role: XH534, XH537, XH558, XH560, XH563, XJ780, XJ782, XJ523 and XJ525. They were delivered between 1973 and early 1977 to No. 27 Squadron, which had just re-formed at RAF Waddington. They were given a high-gloss paint finish to protect against sea-spray effects. The TFR was deleted but aircraft were given the LORAN navigation aid. Five aircraft were further modified for the air-sampling role, taking over from the Handley Page Victor SR2 of No. 543 Squadron. They retained the gloss finish with light grey undersides when the B.Mk2 Vulcans were given a matt all-surface camouflage.

Air monitoring

The air-monitoring system was used for the detection and collection of radioactive particles from the upper atmosphere. The system combined four separate functions:

1. Radiation detection
2. Collection and density monitoring
3. Sample collection of radioactive particles
4. Cabin air sampling

Two pods were fitted with sampling pods using the de Havilland Sea Vixen drop tanks, which used the mounting points that would have carried the Skybolt missile. The drawings shown opposite are from AP 101B-1902-1C, dated April 1976.

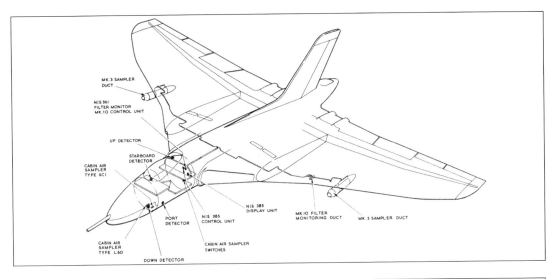

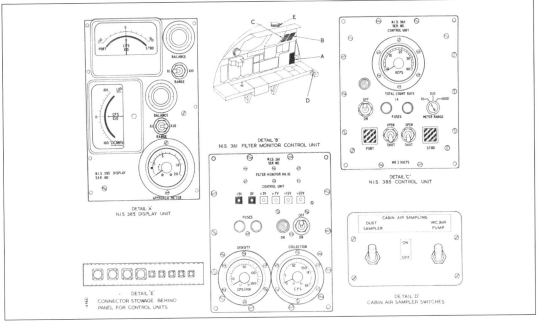

LORAN-C

LORAN-C was a hyperbolic radio navigation system using low-frequency radio signals transmitted by fixed land-based radio beacons to provide a signal that was both long range and highly accurate.

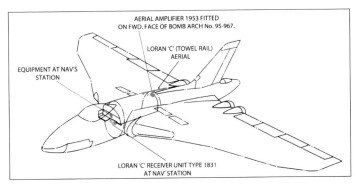

Celebration of 25 Years in Service

To celebrate 25 years in service with the RAF, an exhibition and display was held at RAF Scampton on 25 July 1981. These pictures were taken at that event by Avro photographer Geof Newton, who was Paul Cullerne's deputy at that time.

The flying display included a four-aircraft scramble, after which the Vulcans separated with three aircraft of the Scampton wing making a number of formation flypasts before finally peeling off for a stream landing. Another aircraft from No. 617 'Dambusters' Squadron treated the crowd to a fine solo flying display with some spirited manoeuvres. Norman Barber, the managing director of the then Manchester division of British Aerospace presented the RAF with a fine action painting of the Vulcan.

Operation *Corporate*

It must not be forgotten the contribution made by the Chadderton and Woodford factures in Operation *Corporate*. This not only included the Vulcan but the Victor tanker conversion and Nimrod, which was used in the communications and reconnaissance roles. Weapons and system trials continued throughout the life of the Vulcan, with a variety of options looked at including the dropping of laser-guided bombs.

The Falklands conflict

During the Falklands campaign in 1982, the Vulcan was successfully equipped with the American AGM-45A Shrike anti-radar missile, with two carried under each wing. Shrike missiles managed to hit two targets during the conflict. Flight trials were also attempted with the Anglo-French Martel anti-radiation missile, which was already carried in stock by the RAF for the Blackburn Buccaneer low-level strike aircraft, along with the Westinghouse AN/ALQ-101(V) ECM pod, which provided additional electronic counter measures. These were fitted to improvised pylons on the Vulcan's wings using the Skybolt hard points. To navigate across the huge ocean, the Delco Carousel inertial navigation system was borrowed from the Vickers Super VC10 airliner, with two installed in each Vulcan.

In 1981, the run-down of the Vulcan force had begun with the disbanding of No. 230 OCU on 30 June 1981 at RAF Waddington. One of the first squadrons to lose its Vulcans was No. 617 Squadron, when it finished operating the Vulcan on 31 December 1981. It later converted to the Panavia Tornado GR1 in January 1983.

Six Vulcans were originally chosen for Operation *Black Buck* from the last remaining Vulcan squadrons based at RAF Waddington. The aircraft nominated were to be fitted with Olympus 301 engines, which had been uprated to 20,000lb thrust as it was assumed they would all be equipped with the Skybolt hard points. It was found that XM654 had no hard points, so only five were made available; these were XL391, XM597, XM598, XM607 and XM612. These aircraft had to be converted to the full conventional bombing role and due to lack of use, the refuelling probes had to be reactivated. Intensive crew training ensued, with practice dropping of a full bomb load of 21 1,000lb bombs, flight refuelling and crew procedures.

Issues were encountered with fuel spillage when flight refuelling and various modifications were made by the RAF. To help solve this problem, gutters, deflector plates and vortex generators were fitted forward of the windscreen, but without success. The problem was eventually solved by Flight Refuelling Limited. The aircraft were also given a non-standard dark aircraft grey undersurface camouflage.

Black Buck Missions

Of the seven Operation *Black Buck* missions organised, five were actually flown from Ascension Island in the South Atlantic Ocean. They flew some 7,800 nautical miles with a total flying time of 16 hours. Supported by Victor K2 tankers, the Vulcan was refuelled seven times on the outward journey and once on the return journey. A Nimrod aircraft provided navigation and communications back-up.

The first mission is perhaps the most famous, known as *Black Buck 1*. Captained by Flight Lieutenant Martin Withers, aided by his crew, XM607 dropped a stick of 21 1,000lb bombs on Stanley Airfield, damaging the airport tower and scoring a single direct hit in the centre of the runway. The last *Black Buck* mission was also flown by XM607 against radar installations, using a full load of 1,000lb HE and anti-personnel air-burst bombs.

It is interesting to note that Argentina had considered purchasing the Vulcan on its retirement for the Fuerza Aérea Argentina, which was still operating the Canberra bomber. A majority of the aircraft and equipment used by Argentina was supplied by the United States, France, Italy and the United Kingdom before the conflict began. Most of the equipment was already obsolete but still effective as weapons systems. After more than two decades of service, the Vulcan had not only proved a useful deterrent but in its swan song it was still capable of providing the RAF with a capability beyond its years.

During the Falklands conflict, six Vulcans were converted to the airborne-refuelling role. They were operated by No. 50 Squadron in support of UK air defence operations. Additional fuel was carried in three large tanks fitted in the bomb bay, giving a total fuel capacity of 100,000lb. Shown here is XM571's trailing refuelling probe on 13 July 1982. To aid refuelling, red semi-fluorescent stripes were provided on a white satin-finish undersurface.

Evening flight, XH588 takes off from Woodford, 17 September 1982. Note the sampling pods under the wing along with the hose drum refuelling unit.

Fifty-day wonder

At the start of the Falklands War, British Aerospace's Woodford and Chadderton factories were heavily involved in providing refuelling capabilities for the Nimrod to support missions to the Falklands. Not long after the need arose to make Nimrods capable of in-flight refuelling, the RAF also required more tanker aircraft to supplement the hard-pressed Victor force operating intensively in support of the Falkland Islands operations. The idea of using Vulcans was discussed at Woodford on 30 April 1982, and the feasibility was established during the May bank holiday weekend. The go-ahead was given on Tuesday 4 May 1982, and 50 days later, on Wednesday 23 June, the initial C(A) release to service was given and the first Vulcan tanker, XH561, was delivered to the RAF at Waddington.

At first it was thought it might take only three weeks to prepare the first flight but the decision to mount a hose drum unit (HDU) in the former ECM bay of the Vulcan meant the removal of much of its support structure and a consequently large amount of detail stiffening of the remainder. The HDU had to be split in order to fit it into the aircraft, but the choice of position allowed a third cylindrical tank to be put in the bomb bay to increase the disposable fuel load. The aircraft fuel system was modified to enable bomb bay tanks to be topped up in flight; the bomb bay heating air supply was adapted to drive the HDU fuel pump and condition the HDU bay. Also, electrical supplies were run for HDU and associated equipment.

The whole job involved design groups in both Nimrod and development design centres supported especially by Structures and Mechanical Systems and Avionics. Detail manufacture was undertaken at both Woodford and Chadderton with help from British Aerospace's Warton division and Flight Refuelling Ltd helped with the redesign of the HDU to make it fit in the Vulcan.

Royal Air Force assistance

A fairing to cover the HDU was the only outward sign of the Vulcan's change in role and this was built in No. 3 Work Centre at Chadderton, which handled the strip and modification to the airframes. Especially welcomed to the Manchester team was the first-class assistance from RAF Vulcan crew chiefs, backed by WO Dan Barker of the Nimrod Liaison Office.

Throughout the design, manufacture and assembly, a tremendous effort was maintained. When it came to flight testing, it was disappointing not to have the hose trailed during the first flight on Friday 18 June. However, it was the turn of the flight departments with A&AEE Boscombe Down plus RAF Vulcan crew members to put some hours in and the culmination of a five-day development effort was the passing of fuel to a Victor tanker and a Vulcan bomber aircraft after 'dry' contact with a Nimrod from Woodford, all on the same flight.

Night illumination tests were completed later. Coming, as it did, straight after the effort on Nimrods, this considerable task might fairly be called a 50-day wonder. The 'impossible' task on the Nimrod was done immediately and the Vulcan 'miracle' took a little longer.

The additional fuel load in the Vulcan K2 was carried in three standard Vulcan long-range tanks, which were fitted in the bomb bay. This gave a total fuel capacity of 100,000lb. Six Vulcans were then commissioned into service with No. 50 Squadron from 1982 to 1984. The squadron's principal role was the provision of air-to-air refuelling (AAR) for the UK's air defence, but it also carried out MRR and the air-sampling role.

Vulcans XH558 and XH560, embodying Mod 2390 parts A&B air-monitoring pods and Mod 2600 tanker conversion (Mk17 HDU), were not permitted to use combined operations in the tanker dispensing and air-monitoring mode. For both wet and dry contact dispensing operations, the air-monitoring pods were removed before flight.

Six Vulcan B.Mk2 aircraft were converted to the tanker role; they were XH561, XJ825, XM571, XL445 and B.Mk2 (MRR) XH560 and XH558. The aircraft remained in service with No. 50 Squadron until the unit disbanded on 31 March 1984. It was the last squadron to fly the Vulcan. It was replaced by the Vickers VC10, which had been converted to the AAR role.

Refuelling Tornado, 22 November 1982.

Close-up of the HDU on XH558 at Woodford, 21 September 1982. XH558 also retained its MRR capability.

XH560 refuelling a Lightning interceptor.

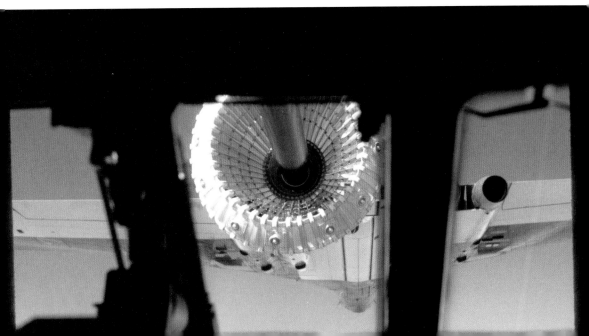

Bomb bay fuel tanks

Various combinations were available using the bay fuel tanks.

Bay Fuel System Tanks A and E		
Tank A (forward or aft position)	596lb	718 gallons (SG 0.77)
Tank E	654lb	721 gallons (SG 0.77)
Tanks A and E	11,081.0lb	1,439 gallons (SG 0.77)

Cylindrical Tanks		
Cylindrical tanks (forward)	7,767lb	1,008.75 gallons
Cylindrical tank (aft)	7,767lb	1,008.75 gallons
Total fuel	15,534lb	2,017.5 gallons (SG 0.77)

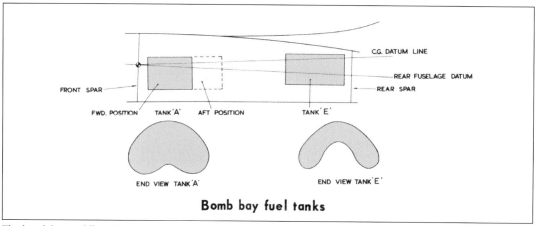

Bomb bay fuel tanks

The bomb bay saddle tanks were built to fit around the Blue Steel missile.

Fuel CG indicator

This instrument was mainly for use during flight refuelling, to aid the pilot to keep the aircraft in longitudinal trim. It showed any variation in the mean fuel CG due to uneven distribution. The gauge was calibrated about the mean CG of the fuel and was connected to the tank contents transmitters via a computer box that took into consideration the moment arm of each tank. The limit of each green sector represents 30,000lb ft out of balance moments, giving a total of 60,000lb ft for the aircraft. When fuel is correctly distributed, the needles are in the middle of the green sector, i.e. the number of out-of-balance moments is zero.

NOTE: This instrument did not give the aircraft CG position and did not include the bomb bay fuel system.

Fuel was carried in 14 bag-type tanks. Port and starboard tanks 1–7 contained 9,260 gallons AVTAG (NATO Code F-40, USA JP4) – SG 0.8 or 9,400 gallons using AVTUR (NATO Code F-34, USA JP8) 40/50 SG 0.77 / 0.78. The weight of the fuel depended on the specific gravities (SG) of the type used.

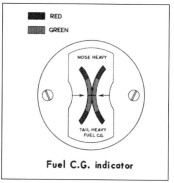

Fuel C.G. indicator

Fuel CG Indicator.

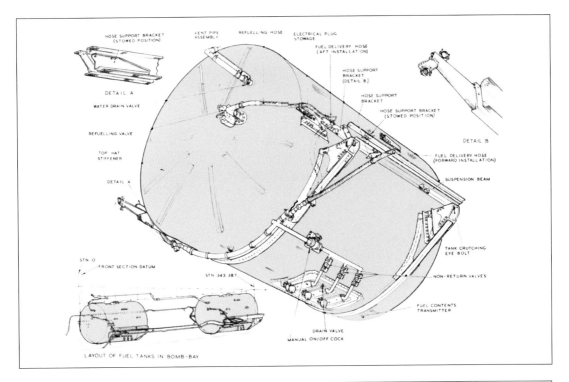

LAYOUT OF FUEL TANKS IN BOMB-BAY

Shown below, three long-range fuel tanks were used on the tanker version of the Vulcan. This gave an extra fuel capacity of 23,301lb.

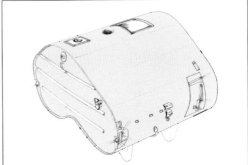

Saddle tank 'A' gave an extra 596lb of fuel.

Fitting the HDU on XH581, used for the air tanker version of the Vulcan.

B.Mk2 Vulcan General Arrangement – 1960

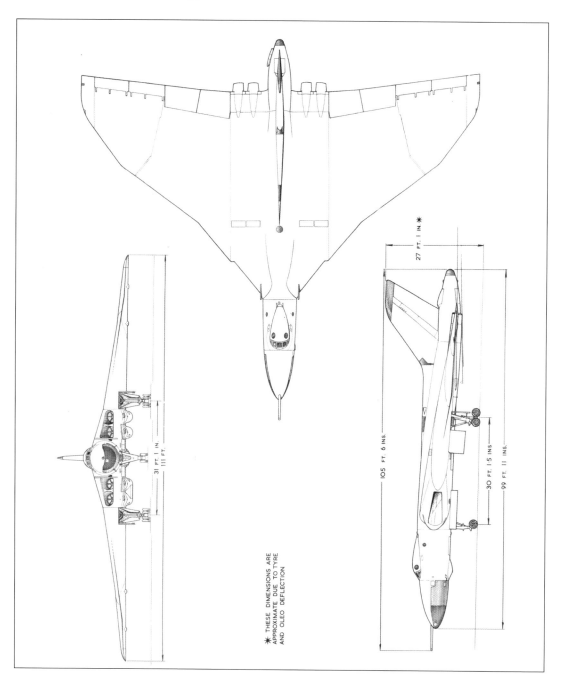

※ THESE DIMENSIONS ARE APPROXIMATE DUE TO TYRE AND OLEO DEFLECTION

31 FT. I IN.
111 FT.

27 FT. I IN. ※

105 FT. 6 INS.

30 FT. 1.5 INS.

99 FT. 11 INS.

Weights and dimensions B.Mk2

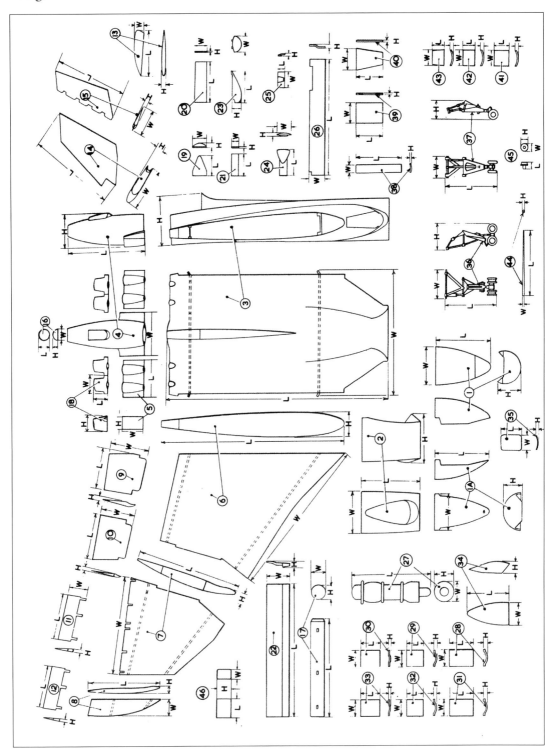

Weights and dimensions B.Mk2 continued

ITEM	COMPONENT	LENGTH (ft)	WIDTH (ft)
1	NOSE (lower portion, composite)	13.5	8.75
1a	NOSE (upper portion, metal)	13.5	8.7
2	FRONT FUSELAGE	16.75	9.2
3	CENTRE SECTION	52.85	28.85
4	REAR FUSELAGE	18.5	10.6
5	REAR FUSELAGE FAIRING	8.25	5.0
6	WING INNER (starboard)	50.0	35.5
6a	WING INNER (port)	50.0	35.5
7	WING OUTER (port and starboard)	24.5	20.5
8	WING TIP (port and starboard)	14.8	3.75
9	ELEVON INNER (inboard, port and starboard)	9.75	10.6
10	ELEVON INNER (outboard, port and starboard)	10.25	8.75
11	ELEVON OUTER (inboard, port and starboard)	9.75	4.25
12	ELEVON OUTER (outboard, port and starboard)	9.75	4.25
13	FIN CAP	11.33	2.25
14	FIN	21.0	10.0
15	RUDDER	19.25	6.0
16	TAIL RADOME	2.47	24.7
17	JET PIPE	22.98	2.63
18	JET PIPE CAP	3.25	4.25
19	FAIRING (counterpoise plate, each)	4.0	3.58
20	COUNTERPOISE PLATE, FRONT (each)	7.6	3.08
20a	COUNTERPOISE PLATE, REAR (each)	5.75	3.25
21	SPLITTER PLATE FRONT (each)	3.87	1.75
21a	SPLITTER PLATE REAR (each)	5.75	2.54
22	BOMB BAY DOORS (each)	29.25	5.2
23	EXPENDABLE FAIRING	7.5	3.75
24	BOMB BAY FAIRING, REAR	6.33	3.25
25	BOMB BAY FAIRING, FRONT	6.0	7.0
26	130MB BAY FAIRING, PORT	29.0	4.75
26a	BOMB BAY FAIRING, STARBOARD	29.0	5.75
27	ENGINE (Olympus 20101) (including oil and starter)	13.68	3.75
28	ENGINE DOOR, FORWARD (inboard, port and stbd)	5.29	4.08
29	ENGINE DOOR, CENTRE (inboard, port and stbd)	4.85	4.04
30	ENGINE DOOR, REAR (inboard, port and stbd)	5.83	4.79
31	ENGINE DOOR, FORWARD (outboard, port and stbd)	5.29	4.08
32	ENGINE DOOR, CENTRE (outboard, port and stbd)	4.83	4.08
33	ENGINE DOOR, REAR (outboard, port and stbd)	5.83	4.79
34	CANOPY	10.5	4.66
35	MAIN ENTRANCE DOOR	5.0	2.75
36	MAIN WHEEL UNIT (each)	12.75	5.0
37	NOSE WHEEL UNIT	13.5	3.5
38	NOSE WHEEL DOOR (each)	10.75	1.75
39	MAIN WHEEL DOOR	6.5	4.75
40	MAIN WHEEL FAIRING	5.25	4.0
41	REAR FUSELAGE ACCESS DOOR (front)	4.27	4.04
42	REAR FUSELAGE ACCESS DOOR (centre)	3.29	4.08
43	REAR FUSELAGE ACCESS DOOR (rear)	3.25	4.0
44	REFUELLING PROBE	9.7	0.5
45	RAM AIR TURBINE	1.3	1.16
46	AIRBORNE AUXILIARY POWER PLANT	4.5	2.0

ITEM	COMPONENT	HEIGHT (ft)	STRUCTURE (tare weight lb)
1	NOSE (lower portion, composite)	5.5	290
1a	NOSE (upper portion, metal)	4.25	230
2	FRONT FUSELAGE	10.25	2,081
3	CENTRE SECTION	12.0	17,979
4	REAR FUSELAGE	6.33	962
5	REAR FUSELAGE FAIRING	3.33	258
6	WING INNER (starboard)	5.0	6,457
6a	WING INNER (port)	5.0	6,446
7	WING OUTER (port and starboard)	2.5	1,708
8	WING TIP (port and starboard)	0.79	107
9	ELEVON INNER (inboard, port and starboard)	1.66	326
10	ELEVON INNER (outboard, port and starboard)	1.5	323
11	ELEVON OUTER (inboard, port and starboard)	1.6	210
12	ELEVON OUTER (outboard, port and starboard)	1.6	203
13	FIN CAP	1.41	80
14	FIN	1.87	919
15	RUDDER	1.0	305
16	TAIL RADOME	1.54	14
17	JET PIPE	2.63	492
18	JET PIPE CAP	2.87	97
19	FAIRING (counterpoise plate, each)	0.5	17
20	COUNTERPOISE PLATE, FRONT (each)	0.08	39
20a	COUNTERPOISE PLATE, REAR (each)	0.08	31
21	SPLITTER PLATE FRONT (each)	0.16	10
21a	SPLITTER PLATE REAR (each)	0.16	23
22	BOMB BAY DOORS (each)	0.66	713
23	EXPENDABLE FAIRING	1.0	60
24	BOMB BAY FAIRING, REAR	1.0	23
25	BOMB BAY FAIRING, FRONT	0.75	4.8
26	BOMB BAY FAIRING, PORT	1.5	444
26a	BOMB BAY FAIRING, STARBOARD	1.6	520
27	ENGINE (Olympus 20101) (including oil and starter)	4.35	4,761
28	ENGINE DOOR, FORWARD (inboard, port and stbd)	0.5	54
29	ENGINE DOOR, CENTRE (inboard, port and stbd)	1.33	80
30	ENGINE DOOR, REAR (inboard, port and stbd.)	1.25	68
31	ENGINE DOOR, FORWARD (outboard, port and stbd)	0.5	52
32	ENGINE DOOR, CENTRE (outboard, port and stbd)	1.33	82
33	ENGINE DOOR, REAR (outboard, port and stbd)	1.25	73
34	CANOPY	1.4	284
35	MAIN ENTRANCE DOOR	1.0	100
36	MAIN WHEEL UNIT (each)	6.0	2,485
37	NOSE WHEEL UNIT	3.08	990
38	NOSE WHEEL DOOR (each)	0.33	48
39	MAIN WHEEL DOOR	0.75	164
40	MAIN WHEEL FAIRING	0.41	32
41	REAR FUSELAGE ACCESS DOOR (front)	0.79	27
42	REAR FUSELAGE ACCESS DOOR (centre)	0.79	23
43	REAR FUSELAGE ACCESS DOOR (rear)	0.87	22
44	REFUELLING PROBE	0.5	38
45	RAM AIR TURBINE	1.25	94
46	AIRBORNE AUXILIARY POWER PLANT	3.16	420

Callsign Avro One

Avro One was the callsign assigned to the Chief Test Pilot at Manchester.

Avro/Manchester Chief Test Pilots	
A V Roe	1908–10
C H Pixton	1911
Lieut W Parke RN	1912
F P Raynham	1913–16
Capt H A Hammersley	1919–21
H J L Hinkler	1921–27
Capt H A Brown	1928–45
S A Thorn	1945–47
J H Orrell	1947–55
R J Falk	1955–58
J G Harrison	1959–70
A L Blackman	1970–78
C B G Masefield	1978–81
J A Robinson	1981–87
P Henley	1987–93
A A McDicken	1993–98
J E Davies	1998
J W A Bolton	1998–2000
A A McDicken	2000–03
J Turner (based at Warton)	

Conclusion of the RAF Vulcan display flight

On 23 March 1993, XH558 made a farewell flypast to the workforce at Woodford before going to Bruntingthorpe for a final display to the public after being retired by the RAF Vulcan Display Flight.

A welcoming sight to many an air crew was Lincoln Cathedral, an indicator that they were close to returning to base. When this picture was taken of XM575 on 10 August 1982, it was flown by Flt Lt Martin Withers, who flew the first *Black Buck* mission in the Falklands campaign. This Vulcan can be seen at the East Midland Aeropark, Castle Donnington, Leicestershire.

Principal suppliers

The manufacture of the Vulcan required a number of UK companies to supply materials and equipment. Shown below are some of the principal suppliers:

T I Aluminium Ltd; Automotive Products Co Ltd; Avica Equipment Ltd: Bell's Asbestos and Engineering Ltd; Belling and Lee Ltd; Birmetals Ltd; Birmingham Aluminium Castings Co Ltd; Thomas Bolton and Sons Ltd; Thomas Boom and Co Ltd; James Booth and Co Ltd; Boulton Paul Aircraft Ltd; British Aluminium Co Ltd; British Electric Resistance Co Ltd; British Insulated Callender's Cables Ltd; British Thomson-Houston Co Ltd; Brown Bayley Steels Ltd; Cellon Ltd; Deritend Drop Forgings Ltd; Diamond H Switches Ltd; Dowty Equipment Ltd; Dunlop Rubber Co Ltd; Dzus Fasteners (Europe) Ltd; English Steel Rolling Mills Corp Ltd; Ferranti Ltd; Fireproof Tanks Ltd; Firth-Vickers Stainless Steels Ltd; Thos Firth and John Brown Ltd; Flight Refuelling Ltd; S Fox and Co Ltd; Hellerman Ltd; High Duty Alloys Ltd; Hymatic Engineering Co Ltd; General Electric Co Ltd; Sir George Godfrey and Partners Ltd; Graviner Manufacturing Co Ltd; Marconi's Wireless Telegraph Co Ltd; Marston Excelsior Ltd; Martin Baker Aircraft Co Ltd; Miller Aviation Ltd; Normalair Ltd; Northern Aluminium Co Ltd; Palmer Aero Products Ltd; Plessey Co Ltd; Pulsometer Engineering Co Ltd; Rotax Ltd; Rubery Owen and Co Ltd; Sangamo Weston Ltd; Self Priming Pumps and Engineering Co Ltd; Smiths Aircraft Instruments Ltd; Simmonds Aerocessories Ltd; Standard Telephones and Cables Ltd; J Stone and Co Ltd; Teddington Aircraft Controls Ltd; Teleflex Products Ltd; Herbert Terry and Sons Ltd; Triplex Safety Glass Co Ltd; Tungum and Co Ltd; and Vickers-Armstrongs Ltd.

Vulcan survivors

XH558	Based at Doncaster Sheffield Airport. Taxiable. Future under review.
XJ823	Solway Aviation Museum, Cumbria.
XJ824	Imperial War Museum, Duxford, Cambridgeshire.
XL318	Royal Air Force Museum, Hendon, London.
XL319	North East Aircraft Museum, Sunderland.
XL361	Goose Bay, Canada.
XL426	London Southend Airport. Taxiable.
XM573	Strategic Air and Space Museum, US.
XM575	East Midland Aeropark, Castle Donnington, Leicestershire.
XM594	Newark Air Museum Nottinghamshire.
XM598	RAF Museum, Cosford, Midlands.
XM603	Avro Heritage Museum, Woodford, Cheshire.
XM605	Castle Air Museum, US.
XM607	RAF Waddington, Lincoln, Lincolnshire.
XM612	City of Norwich Aviation Museum Norfolk.
XM655	Wellesborne, Warwickshire Mounford Airfield. Taxiable.

Pictured at the Woodford Airshow are XH558 and XM603.

Woodford's Own Vulcan – XM603

Inset: Pictured with XM603 on its last flight, (Sir) Charles Masefield, who later became the general manager of the Manchester division, and Bob Pogson (left) and Ted Hartley (right) – both survivors of the Vulcan XA891 crash in 1959.

Avro Vulcan XM603 on its last flight. It can be seen at the Avro Heritage Museum in its original all-white anti-flash colour scheme.

Vulcan B.Mk2 Production

August 1957

The second prototype Vulcan VX777 first flew with the Phase 2C wing used by the B.Mk2 Vulcan on 31 August 1957.

1958

XH533: C/N. Set No. 1. First flight: 30 August 1958. Olympus 200 engines. Used for manufacturing trials including automatic landing trials in 1961. Sold for scrap to Bradbury & Co in 1970.

1959

XH536: C/N. Set No. 4. First flight: 3 May 1959. Delivered: July 1959. Olympus 201 engines. Used for TFR trials. Crashed at Fan Bwlch Chwyth in the Brecon Beacons in Wales on 11 February 1966 while on a TFR training flight in bad weather at low attitude. All five crew were killed.

XH534: C/N. Set No. 2. First flight: 18 June 1959. Delivered: 5 December 1966. Olympus 201 engines. Used for manufacturing trials. The first Vulcan B.Mk2 fitted with the new counter measure suite. Converted to the MRR and air-sampling role. Scrapped in February 1982.

1960

XH557: C/N. Set No. 11. First flight: 2 April 1960. Delivered: 3 December 1965. Fitted with Olympus 201 engines. Converted with Olympus 301 engines and the first to have enlarged intakes. Scrapped in December 1982.

XH535: C/N. Set No. 3. First flight: 7 May 1960. Delivered: 27 May 1960. Olympus 201 engines. Used for manufacturing trials, which included the Skybolt ballistic missile. Used for ECM and window trials at the A&AEE between the 5 May 1960 and 5 May 1964. Crashed due to engine stall at Chute near Andover on 11 May 1964, with four fatalities from the crew of six. The pilots ejected and survived.

XH558: C/N. Set No. 12. First flight: 25 May 1960. Delivered: 1 June 1960. Olympus 201 engines. In November 1975, during take-off, the No. 3 engine disintegrated after ingesting a seagull. Subsequent major repairs meant the aircraft was grounded for many years and led to significantly fewer flying hours than most Vulcans. Converted to the MRR and air-sampling role and later to the K2 tanker role. Struck off charge in March 1993. The aircraft became the last Vulcan to fly due to public demand and retired in 2015. The aircraft is now on static display at Doncaster Sheffield Airport, Doncaster.

XH559: C/N. Set No. 13. First flight: 29 June 1960. Delivered: 24 August 1960. Olympus 201 engines. Sold for scrap and scrapped in February 1982.

XH537: C/N. Set No. 5. First flight: 4 August 1960. Delivered: 28 May 1965. Olympus 201 engines. Used for manufacturer's and Skybolt-missile-dropping trials. Converted to the MRR and air-sampling role in 1978. Went to Abingdon in 1983 to be used as an instructional airframe. Scrapped in May 1991. The nose was saved and bought by Colin Mears. In March 2003, the aircraft was sold to the Bournemouth Aviation Museum at Bournemouth Airport, Hurn, Dorset.

XH560: C/N. Set No. 14. First flight: 30 August. Delivered: September 1960. Olympus 201 engines. Converted to the MRR and air-sampling role, then later to the K2 tanker role. Scrapped November 1984.

XH561: C/N. Set No. 15. First flight: 17 September 1960. Delivered: October 1960. Olympus 201 engines. Converted to the K2 tanker role. Sent to firefighting school at Catterick in 1984.

XH562: C/N. Set No. 16. First flight: 21 October 1960. Delivered: November 1960. Olympus 201 engines. Sent to firefighting school at Catterick during August 1982.

XH563: C/N. Set No. 17. First flight: 1 November 1960. Delivered: December 1960. Olympus 201/301 engines. Modified to the MRR and air-sampling role. Sent to Scampton for preservation in 1982. Scrapped at St Athan on 28 July 1986.

XJ780: C/N. Set No. 18. First flight: 28 November 1960. Delivered: January 1961. Olympus 201 engines. Converted to the MRR role in 1976. Used for spares before being scrapped in 1982.

1961

XH538: C/N. Set No. 6. First flight: 4 January 1961. Delivered: 30 January 1961. Olympus 201 engines. Joined the RAF in 1965. Used for Blue Steel trials and modified for the Skybolt ballistic missile. Remained with the MoA until 1965. Converted to the MRR role. Finally sent to St Athan and scrapped in August 1981.

XJ781: C/N. Set No. 19. First flight: 10 January 1961. Delivered: 22 January 1961. Olympus 201 engines. Damaged during landing at Shiraz in Iran when the port undercarriage failed to lower due to hydraulic failure on 23 May 1973. Damaged beyond repair and struck off charge 1973.

XJ782: C/N. Set No. 20. First flight: 16 January 1961. Delivered: 22 February 1961. Olympus 201 engines. Converted to the MRR role. Sent to Finningley for preservation but later scrapped in 1988.

XJ783: C/N. Set No. 21. First flight: 3 February 1961. Delivered: 10 March 1961. Olympus 201 engines. Withdrawn from service in 1982. Used for spares recovery and sold for scrap in November 1982.

XH554: C/N. Set No. 8. First flight: 18 February 1961. Delivered: 7 April 1961. Olympus 201 engines. Sent to firefighting school at Catterick in 1981. Scrapped in February 1984.

XJ784: C/N. Set No. 22. First flight: 9 March 1961. Delivered: 21 December 1966. Olympus 201 engines. Converted with 301 engines and went to the A&AEE in April 1962 for initial C(A) release trials. Sold for scrap in 1982 after spares recovery.

XJ823: C/N. Set No. 23. First flight: 30 March 1961. Delivered 20 April 1961. Olympus 201 engines. Sold to Solway Aviation Society in Carlisle January 1983.

XJ824: C/N. Set No. 24. First flight: 24 April 1961. Delivered: 15 May 1961. Olympus 201 engines. Sent to the Imperial War Museum, Duxford, for display in March 1982.

XH539: C/N. Set No. 7. First flight: 10 May 1961. Delivered: September 25 May 1961. Olympus 201 engines. Used for Blue Steel manufacturing trials. Later sent to Waddington fire dump on 7 March 1972. Scrapped in 1989.

XH555: C/N. Set No. 3. First flight: 9 June 1961. Delivered: 14 July 1961. Olympus 201 engines. The aircraft had a heavy landing at Finningley in 1968. It was then used for fatigue tests at Woodford until 1970. Scrapped in 1977.

XL317: C/N. Set No. 26. First flight: 24 June 1961. Delivered: 1 December 1962. Olympus 201 engines. It was the first Blue Steel aircraft delivered to the RAF. Sent to Akrotiri, Cyprus, before being scrapped in 1987.

XJ825: C/N. Set No. 25. First flight: 7 July 1961. Delivered: 27 July 1961. Converted to the MRR role in 1976. Used for battle damage repair duties before being scrapped in 1992 at Waddington.

XL318: C/N. Set No. 27. First flight: 11 August 1961. Delivered: 1 September 1961. Olympus 201 engines. Modified for the Blue Steel missile. Used for the last Vulcan sortie by 617 Squadron. Went to the RAF Museum London at Hendon, on 12 February 1982.

XH556: C/N. Set No. 10. First flight: 31 August 1961. Delivered: 26 September 1961. Olympus 201 engines. Withdrawn after undercarriage collapsed on 18 April 1966 at Finningley due to an engine fire during start-up. Used for fire practice.

XL319: C/N. Set No. 28. First flight: 1 October 1961. Delivered: 20 October 1961. Olympus 201 engines. Modified for Blue Steel. It was the second B.Mk2 delivered to 617 Squadron. Sold to North East Land, Sea and Air Museums at the former Sunderland Airport, now a Nissan car factory. Flew from Waddington to the museum on 21 January 1983.

XL320: C/N. Set No. 29. First flight: 9 November 1961. Delivered: 1 December 1961. Olympus 201 engines. Modified for Blue Steel missile. Scrapped at St Athan in 1981.

XL321: C/N. Set No. 30. First flight: 6 December 1961. Delivered: 10 January 1962. Olympus 201 engines. It had the highest number of operational flying hours of a Vulcan, with more than 6,952 hours recorded. Went to Catterick fire school. Perished in 1987.

1962

XL359: C/N. Set No. 31. First flight: 10 January 1962. Delivered: 1 February 1962. Olympus 201 engines. Modified for Blue Steel. Allocated as gate guardian for RAF Scampton. Scrapped in November 1982.

XL360: C/N. Set No. 32. First flight: 31 January 1962. Delivered: 1 March 1962. Olympus 201/301 engines. Modified for Blue Steel missile. Sold in 1983 to Midland Air Museum.

XL361: C/N. Set No. 33. First flight: 21 February 1962. Delivered: 14 March 1962. Olympus 201 engines. Modified for Blue Steel missile. Had an accident at Happy Valley-Goose Bay, Canada, during 1981 that led to fire damage of the main electrical loom and the aircraft was written off. Permission was given in March 1982 for the aircraft to be put on display at Goose Bay.

XL384: C/N. Set No. 34. First flight: 16 March 1962. Delivered: 31 January 1962. Olympus 301 engines. Conversion to Blue Steel role. Damaged after heavy landing on 12 August 1971. Used for crash rescue training. Struck off charge in 1985. Scrapped at Scampton.

XL385: C/N. Set No. 35. First flight: 30 March 1962. Delivered: 17 April 1962. Olympus 201/301 engines. Conversion to Blue Steel missile role, including fitting of 301 engines. At the start of a take-off run from Scampton, the No. 1 engine exploded, with debris rupturing the fuel tanks. The aircraft was destroyed by fire. Struck off charge on 6 April 1967.

XL386: C/N. Set No. 36. First flight: 2 May 1962. Delivery date: 11 May 1962. Olympus 201 engines. Conversion to Blue Steel missile role, including fitting of 301 engines. Delivered to Central Training Establishment, Manston, Kent, August 1982. Scrapped at Manston in 1994.

XL387: C/N. Set No. 37. First flight: 16 May 1962. Delivered: 1 June 1962. Olympus 201/301 engines Conversion to Blue Steel missile role including fitting of 301 engines. Sent to St Athan for crash rescue training in January 1982. Sold for scrap in June 1983.

XL388: C/N. Set No. 38. First flight: 25 May 1962. Delivered: 13 June 1962. Olympus 201/301 engines. Conversion to Blue Steel missile role, including fitting of 301 engines. Sent to Honington fire dump in August 1982. Scrapped in 1985. Nose section sent to South Yorkshire Aircraft Museum.

XL389: C/N. Set No. 39. First flight: 13 June 1962. Delivered: 11 July 1962. Olympus 201/301 engines. Conversion to Blue Steel missile role, including fitting of 301 engines. Scrapped at St Athan on 31 August 1981.

XL390: C/N. Set No. 40. First flight: 3 July 1962. Delivered: 11 August 1962. Olympus 201/301 engines. Conversion to Blue Steel missile role, including fitting of 301 engines. Crashed during an air display at

Northbrook near NAS Glenview, USA, on 11 August 1978 due to a possible stall at around 400ft during wing over. Four fatalities.

XL392: C/N. Set No. 42. First flight: 19 July 1962. Delivered: 1 August 1962. Olympus 201/301 engines. Conversion to Blue Steel missile role, including fitting of 301 engines. Sent to RAF Valley, Anglesey, for crash rescue training in March 1982. Later scrapped in August 1993.

XL425: C/N. Set No. 43. First flight: 6 August 1962. Delivered: 30 August 1962. Olympus 201/301 engines. Conversion to Blue Steel missile role, including fitting of 301 engines. Grounded January 1982. Scrapped April the same year.

XL426: C/N. Set No. 44. First flight: 13 August 1962. Delivered: 12 September 1962. Olympus 201. Conversion to Blue Steel missile role. In 1984, it performed air displays for the public with the RAF Vulcan Display Flight. It was put up for sale in 1986 and purchased by Roy Jacobsen, registered as G-VET in July 1987. It is now run by the Vulcan Restoration Trust based at London Southend Airport.

XL427: C/N. Set No. 45. First flight: 14 September 1962. Delivered: 1 October 1962. Olympus 201/301 engines. Conversion to Blue Steel missile role, including fitting of 301 engines. Used for crash rescue training at RAF Machrihanish, Scotland, from August 1982. Scrapped in 1986.

XL443: C/N. Set No. 46. First flight: 18 September 1962. Delivered: 5 October 1962. Olympus 201/301 engines. Conversion to Blue Steel missile role, including fitting of 301 engines. Allocated to the RAF Museum in 1982 before being sold to the Bird Group as scrap. Scrapped in April 1982.

XL444: C/N. Set No. 47. First flight: 12 October 1962. Delivered: 30 October 1962. Olympus 201 engines. Conversion to the Blue Steel missile role. Grounded September 1982 and scrapped in December 1982.

XL445: C/N. Set No. 48. First flight: 30 October 1962. Delivered: 24 November 1962. Olympus 201 engines. Conversion to Blue Steel missile role. Converted to the K2 tanker role in 1982 and served with 50 Squadron until March 1984. Last used for crash recue training at Lyneham, Wiltshire. Scrapped in 1987. The nose was preserved at RAF Scampton.

XL446: C/N. Set No. 49. First flight: 16 November 1962. Delivered: 29 November 1962. Olympus 201 engines. Conversion to Blue Steel missile role. Grounded in March 1982. Sold to the Bird Group for scrap in November of the same year.

XM569: C/N. Set No. 50. First flight: 11 December 1962. Delivered: 31 January 1963. Olympus 201 engines. Conversion to Blue Steel missile role. Sold to South Wales Aviation Museum. Sent to Cardiff in February 1983. Aircraft scrapped but nose section saved at the Jet Age Museum, Gloucester.

1963

XM570: C/N. Set No. 51. First flight: 31 January 1963. Delivered: 26 February 1963. Olympus 201 engines. Conversion to Blue Steel missile role. Went to St Athan on 10 March 1981. Sold as scrap on 29 January 1982.

XM571: C/N. Set No. 52. First flight: 31 January 1963. Delivered: 21 February 1963. Olympus 201/301 engines. Conversion to the Blue Steel missile role. Converted to the MRR and tanker role. Delivered to Gibraltar for preservation, later scrapped in September 1990.

XM572: C/N. Set No. 53. First flight: 9 February 1963. Delivered: 1 March 1963. Olympus 201 engines. Conversion to the Blue Steel missile role. Grounded in September 1982. Sold to the Bird Group for scrap on 30 November 1982.

XM573: C/N. Set No. 54. First flight: 27 February 1963. Delivered: 27 March 1963. Olympus 201 engines. Sent to Offutt Air Force Base, USA, in 1982. Presented to the USAF on 7 June 1982 and preserved at SAC Museum, Ashland, Nebraska.

XM574: C/N. Set No. 55. First flight: 28 March 1963. Delivered: 17 June 1963. Olympus 301 engines. Conversion to the Blue Steel missile role. Sent to St Athan on 16 December 1981. Scrapped on 29 January 1982.

XM575: C/N. Set No. 56. First flight: 19 April 1963. Delivered: 21 May 1963. Olympus 301 engines. Conversion to Blue Steel missile role. Sold to Leicestershire Air Museum in January 1983. Delivered to Bruntingthorpe. Ferried to Castle Donington, East Midlands Aeropark.

XL391: C/N. Set No. 41. First flight: 14 May 1963. Delivered 22 May 1963. Olympus 301 engines. Reserve aircraft for the *Black Buck* raids on Stanley Airport, Falkland Islands. Sent to Blackpool for display on 16 February 1983. Scrapped in January 2006.

XM576: C/N. Set No. 57. First flight: 16 May 1963. Delivered: 6 June 1963. Olympus 301 engines. Conversion to Blue Steel missile role. Crash landed at Scampton in May 1965 during an asymmetric approach. Damaged beyond repair.

XM594: C/N. Set No. 58. First flight: 4 June 1963. Delivered: 9 July 1963. Olympus 301 engines. Blue Steel missile modifications. Sold in January 1983. Sent to Newark Air Museum, Nottinghamshire, (former RAF Winthorpe) on 7 February 1983. Aircraft preserved.

XM595: C/N. Set No. 59. First flight: 4 July 1963. Delivered: 20 August 1963. Olympus 301 engines. Blue Steel missile modifications. Grounded in March 1982. Scrapped in November 1982.

XM596: C/N. Set No. 60. Based at Woodford and used for static fatigue testing due to change to low-level role. Scrapped in 1972.

XM597: C/N. Set No. 61. First flight: 12 July. Delivered: 27 August 1963. Olympus 301 engines. Blue Steel missile modifications. Testing of passive ECM radar-warning receiver mounted on top of tail between November 1971 and February 1973. Modified for *Black Buck* operations in July 1982. Completed two *Black Buck* missions. On its last mission it diverted to Brazil due to a broken refuelling probe. It was sent to the National Museum of Flight in East Fortune on 12 April 1984. Aircraft preserved.

XM598: C/N. Set No. 62. First flight: 15 August 1963. Delivered: 3 September 1963. Olympus 301 engines. Modified for *Black Buck* operations in July 1982. The aircraft was to perform the first primary mission but was replaced by XM607 due to cabin pressurisation failure. Sent to the RAF Museum Cosford on 20 January 1983.

XM599: C/N. Set No. 63. First flight: 30 August 1963. Delivered: 30 September 1963. Olympus 301 engines. Sold to H John & Co. for scrap in January 1982. Scrapped at St Athan on 29 January 1982.

XM600: C/N. Set No. 64. First flight: 6 September 1963. Delivered: 2 October 1963. Olympus 301 engines. A fire in the bomb bay area spread to the port wing. The crew bailed out near Spilsby, Lincolnshire, on 17 January 1977. (101 Squadron RAF).

XM601: C/N. Set No. 65. First flight: 21 October 1963. Delivered: 4 November 1963. Olympus 301 engines. Destroyed in a crash on approach to Coningsby, Lincolnshire, on 7 October 1963. The wingtip hit the ground on an asymmetric approach; the aircraft overshot and span in due to lack of rudder authority. All five crew were killed.

XM602: C/N. Set No. 66. First flight: 28 October 1963. Delivered: 12 November 1963. Olympus 301 engines. Delivered to St Athan in January 1982. Broken up in September 1992. The nose section was saved and now resides at the Avro Heritage Museum at Woodford, Cheshire.

XM603: C/N. Set No. 67. First flight: 15 November 1963. Delivered: 3 December 1963. Olympus 301 engines. Sold to British Aerospace for preservation. Delivered to Woodford in March 1982. Used as a mock-up for the K2 tanker conversion. Now part of the Avro Heritage Museum as a static exhibit.

XM604: C/N. Set No. 68. First flight: 15 November 1963. Delivered: 4 December 1963. Olympus 301 engines. Overshot the runway and crashed at Cottesmore due to an engine failure on 30 January 1968. Both pilots ejected but four crew were killed.

XM605: C/N. Set No. 69. First flight: 22 November 1963. Delivered: 20 December 1963. Olympus 301 engines. Flew its last sortie on 20 August 1981. Preserved at Castle Air Force Base, USA. Presented to the USAF on 2 September 1981.

XM606: C/N. Set No. 70. First flight: 28 November 1963. Delivered: 20 December 1963. Olympus 301 engines. Retired on 7 June 1982. It was gifted to the 8th Air Force Museum at Barksdale (now Barksdale Global Power Museum) a week later.

XM607: C/N. Set No. 71. First flight: 29 November 1963. Delivered: 31 December 1963. Olympus 301 engines. Modified for Operation *Black Buck*. Completed three missions, including the first one captained by Martin Withers. On static display at Waddington from January 1983.

XM608: C/N. Set No. 72. First flight: 24 December 1963. Delivered: 28 January 1964. Olympus 301 engines. Scrapped by Bird Group in December 1982.

1964

XM609: C/N. Set No. 73. First flight: 2 January 1964. Delivered: 28 January 1964. Olympus 301 engines. Delivered to St Athan in March 1981. Scrapped on 31 August 1981.

XM610: C/N. Set No. 74. First flight: 22 January 1964. Delivered: 11 February 1964. Olympus 301 engines. Crashed near Wingate, County Durham, on 8 January 1971 following a fire in a No. 1 engine bay that spread to the wing fuel tanks. The rear crew parachuted safely; later, the two pilots successfully ejected.

XM611: C/N. Set No. 75. First flight: 23 January 1964. Delivered: 13 February 1964. Olympus 301 engines. Scrapped at St Athan on 2 June 1983.

XM612: C/N. Set No. 76. First flight: 13 February 1964. Delivered: 2 March 1964. Olympus 301 engines. Modified for *Black Buck* missions. Sold to City of Norwich Aviation Museum; delivered on 30 January 1983.

XM645: C/N. Set No. 77. First flight: 25 February 1964. Delivered: 11 March 1964. Olympus 301 engines. It suffered an onboard explosion caused by a heavy landing at Żabbar, Malta, on 14 October 1975. There were five fatalities plus one civilian on the ground. Both pilots ejected and survived. It had a crew of seven.

XM646: C/N. Set No. 78. First flight: 16 March 1964. Delivered: 7 April 1964. Olympus 301 engines. Sold to T Bradbury as scrap. Scrapped at St Athan on 29 June 1982.

XM647: C/N. Set No. 79. First flight: 2 April 1964. Delivered: 15 April 1964. Olympus 301 engines. Used for ground instruction training at RAF Laarbruch, Germany, on 17 September 1982 as 8765M. Scrapped on 1 March 1985.

XM648: C/N. Set No. 80. First flight: 17 April 1964. Delivered: 5 May 1964. Olympus 301 engines. Grounded on 10 September 1982 at RAF Waddington, Lincolnshire. Scrapped on 8 December 1982.

XM649: C/N. Set No. 81. First flight: 28 April 1964. Delivered: 13 May 1964. Olympus 301 engines. Scrapped at St Athan on 2 December 1982.

XM650: C/N. Set No. 82. First flight: 12 May 1964. Delivered: 27 May 1964. In 1972, it was part of the Waddington wing. Scrapped at St Athan in 1984.

XM651: C/N. Set No. 83. First flight: 1 June 1964. Delivered in June 1964. Olympus 301 engines. Grounded at Waddington in September 1982. Scrapped on 30 November 1982.

XM652: C/N. Set No. 84. First flight: 16 July 1964. Delivered on 14 August 1964. Olympus 301 engines. Dismantled in March 1984. Nose section is part of a private collection at a farm in Welshpool.

XM653: C/N. Set No. 85. First flight: 14 August 1964. Delivered on 3 September 1964. Olympus 301 engines. Moved to St Athan before being scrapped in 1981.

XM654: C/N. Set No. 86. First flight: 2 October 1964. Delivered on 22 October 1964. Olympus 301 engines. Grounded in October 1982. Scrapped in November 1982.

XM655: C/N. Set No. 87. First flight: 2 November 1964. Delivered: 20 November 1964. Olympus 301 engines. Retired in 1983. Bought by Roy Jacobson. Sent to Wellesbourne Mountford Aerodrome, Warwickshire, on 11 February 1984. Registered G-VULC and later registered N6655AV. Aircraft preserved.

XM656: C/N. Set No. 88. First flight: 25 November 1964. Delivered on 14 December 1964. Olympus 301 engines. Given to Cottesmore for display. Sold as scrap in 1983.

XM657: C/N. Set No. 89. First flight: 21 December 1964. Delivered: 14 January 1965. Olympus 301 engines. The last Vulcan delivered. Delivered to Manston on 12 January 1982 as an instructional airframe. Scrapped in November 1992.

Vulcan B.Mk2 MRR aircraft
XH534, XH537, XH558, XH560, XH563, XJ780, XJ782, XJ823, XJ825

Vulcan B.Mk2 K2 tankers
XH558, XH560, XH561, XJ825, XL445, XM571

Vulcan B.Mk2s modified to carry Blue Steel missile
XH439, XL317, XL318, XL319, XL320, XL321, XL359, XL360, XL361, XL384, XL385, XL386, XL387, XL388, XL389, XL390, XL392, XL425, XL426, XL427, XL443, XL444, XL445, XL446, XM569, XM570, XM571, XH572, XH574, XL575, XH576, XH594, XH595

Operation *Black Buck* aircraft used in the Falklands conflict
XM598, XM607, XM612, XM597

The B-52 first flew on 5 April 1952, with the final variant, the B-52H, having its first flight on 6 March 1961. The B-52H had a wingspan of 185ft and a length of 157ft 7in and was powered by eight TF-33 turbofan engines of 17,000lb thrust. It had a range of some 10,000 miles, with a ceiling of more than 50,000ft at 650mph; its gross weight was 488,000lb. Production reached 744 aircraft, manufactured by the Boeing Seattle, Washington, and Wichita, Kansas, plants between 1952 and 1962.

It has been announced that the B52 is being upgraded to allow it to remain in service until 2044. The Rolls-Royce F130 will replace the TF30-PW-103, which has powered the B52 since the 1960s.

This picture, taken by Dave Draycot, shows the last flying Vulcan, XH558, at the 2009 Royal International Air Tattoo at Fairford, Gloucestershire. It is seen here with a Boeing B-52H Stratofortress, which is still operated by the USAF Air Combat Command.

Other books you might like:

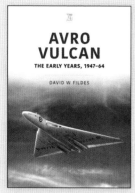

Historic Military Aircraft
Series, Vol. 7

Aviation Industry Series,
Vol. 3

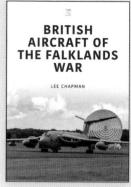

Historic Military Aircraft
Series, Vol. 13

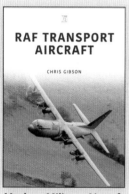

Modern Military Aircraft
Series, Vol. 6

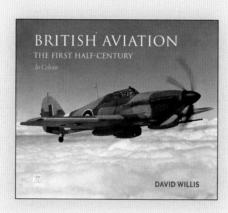

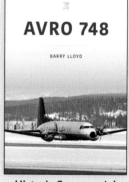

Historic Commercial
Aircraft Series, Vol. 3

For our full range of titles please visit:
shop.keypublishing.com/books